Children Are Like That!

Observations from the Children's Farm

By Nancy Jones

ISBN-13: 978-0-578-48613-0

Printed in the United States of America

Cover photos: Peter Vordenberg

Editor: Jami Carpenter

Contents

Introduction

FOLLOWING ARE STORIES of actual children, ages three to five, who attended a unique school in Minnesota. The Children's Farm was created in 1976 as an alternative to closed indoor classrooms with plastic toys springing up as daycares and learning centers for children. The school is located on a former dairy farm, a small diversified barnyard with chicken coop, pig sty, sheep pen, and granary, located on about sixty acres of rolling pasture, pond, and field.

In this setting early childhood teachers have applied current educational philosophies and research-based methods, even as they took advantage of traditional ways that children learned in former centuries, by learning and playing outdoors as part of a working society.

What we have learned over the last forty years is the subject of this book. Each story has a theme, but like all learning, the areas of development — emotional, social, physical, and cognitive — interact and complement each other. I have tried to show the context of time and place, quoting children who actually said and did these things. The comments I have added to each story are directed at both teachers and parents, because just as we know all parents are teachers of their own children, so in many ways do teachers share in the nurturing of the young children they care for and teach. Our jobs overlap, and so do my comments.

I believe this information is valuable, not because I expect a new wave of 'farm schools,' although a few have sprung up in our developing suburban area as a response to our example. Rather, I think our experience here has allowed us to see what children are capable of, to learn of their strengths. I am concerned that current child development and early childhood researchers are studying the children our society has put to play in boxes with cages behind them, who go home to families where they are amused or technologically entertained, but not challenged or asked to contribute. The accounts of the capabilities of children raised in this way (and those are the ones studied) do not match the inquisitive, confident, and caring children I see each day at our school, nor the ones my husband and I raised in our life together on a farm.

In addition, I see and hope the reader will realize that many of the effective strategies and activities we have developed in teaching children on a farm are also possible in more urban area schools, daycare centers, and daycare homes and can be adapted to fit new settings.

We need to get out of the mold of thinking that 'since schools are like this, children are like this.' Instead, we can say, 'children are like that, so we should have the schools be like that.' We can look for alternatives to the passive, entertainment-based, belittling patterns that I see in many schools and in many families.

The needs of children and the ways in which they learn have not changed, even as we have changed their environments. I invite you to listen to the stories of these children as they remind us again of the needs of all humans to be contributing, learning, and respected members of society. *Children are like that.*

Part 1: Social/Emotional Development

Callie: "... she needs this!"

*A stimulating learning environment
appeals to basic needs of all children.*

I COULD TELL it was another negotiating morning for
Callie. She wouldn't look at me, her teacher. Her small,
smiling face beneath straight carrot-colored bangs was
screwed up into a major pout as she clung tightly to her
mother's hand. This was a child whose mother had trouble
leaving either of her two daughters. At their slightest whine,
Mrs. Linder would cajole and baby-talk, or stay for a while,
even though the teachers had reassured her often that her
daughters settled in happily once she was out of the parking
lot. It seemed to us that it was the parent who lacked
confidence in us and our place. Why, I wondered, had she
chosen our school-on-a-farm for her children?

That day, however, Mrs. Linder seemed determined that
Callie should stay. They had settled on a plea agreement:
Mom would come in and help her daughter go to the
bathroom first. Of course, our teachers can help as well, but
I smiled and agreed. "We'll see you out by the barn." As
Callie and her mother started toward the schoolroom, I led
a cheerful younger sister, Jessica, to join the other children
as they eagerly raced past the farmhouse and tumbled over
the hill toward the barnyard. The animals were fed quickly.
It was a damp, misty day and the children anticipated going
to the hayloft, a popular play place.

Before they'd climb up, however, the teachers had proposed a 'job.' Now that winter sledding days were past, we were to take out the little red wagons, load the hay bales resting beside the sledding hill onto them, and return them to the barn. When Callie and her mother came over the hill, they saw Jessica, along with another three-year-old girl and me, tipping a bale up onto a wagon. We oof-ed and grunted as we pushed. We cheered when we got it on! Callie and her mother helped us navigate it down the hill and into the barn, where we heaved and ho'd and one-two-three'd, and it was stacked by the cement block wall just inside the barn door.

"Now there are four strong women." I said, winking at Mrs. Linder.

Of all the children at our school, her daughters were the most perfectly dressed, clad daily in matching play overalls, color-coordinated from their socks to their hair ribbons. *Why does she send them here?* I thought, as I brushed the hay from my dusty snow pants.

A few weeks earlier Mrs. Linder had informed me that she couldn't enroll the younger sister, Jessica, for school here the next year. With one in kindergarten, the timing and driving distance, surely I understood. Of course I did. "We all have our limits on time and driving," I sympathized. Yet I wondered if perhaps we just weren't quite consistent with her values, either.

The six other children in my charge were now clamoring to climb to the hayloft. I opened the barn gate and they rushed to form a line at the base of the haymow ladder. One by one, they sturdily mounted the rungs of the ladder, pushed off with a step to the side, and disappeared into the loft above where they knew they must wait on the board seats until a teacher climbed up.

"Lines aren't so difficult to practice when they make sense," I told Mrs. Linder as we stood beside the ladder and watched as each child eagerly stepped up. I added that the children needed no reminders to remain seated up above, because they knew we would ask them to climb back down if they so much as budged toward the inviting mounds of hay.

Mrs. Linder smiled and nodded. As each child climbed up in rapid succession, she seemed more and more pleased. It occurred to me that although parents know we play in the hayloft, on another level they really don't understand how competently their children get themselves up there. After all, these are the same parents who lift their kids into their cars at the end of the school day!

At last Jessica and Callie climbed up, Jessica more slowly and deliberately, intent on the job at hand. Callie climbed quickly, looking back with a smile between steps to see if her mother was watching. We adults zipped up next, and at a word from me the children were off and about in the giant cavernous loft — climbing, sliding, balancing on the board 'bridge,' and jumping down into soft beds of hay. Soon a few began pulling together on a bale to push down to the waiting horses below.

Mrs. Linder watched for a few minutes beside me, savoring what must have looked like kid paradise. Then she offered, "I was visiting at another preschool nearer my home this morning, for Jessica next year."

"Ahh …" (not knowing what to say).

"But … it wasn't the same … at all!"

"I guess not," I said, trying to be diplomatic. "Not many haylofts …"

"There were lines, though. A lot of lines. Lines for everything."

I turned to respond to a child whose shoe had come untied. When I came back, to my surprise, I saw tears in Mrs. Linder's eyes. She flushed, tried a smile, and dabbed her face. I looked away, thinking I'd pretend I hadn't noticed, but Mrs.

Linder wanted to continue ...

"Jessica will be okay there. I mean, she likes to do puzzles and cut and paste. But ... this ... she *needs* this ..." she waves her hand toward Callie, now happily bouncing among the frolicking children who had just climbed so heartily up that ladder. "Where else will she get *this*?"

THOUGHTS FOR TEACHERS

The world has changed, and so has the environment our children are living in today.

The world in which we are raising the children of the twenty-first century has changed greatly from the time of just a generation ago when children played in neighborhood yards, climbed trees, helped with chores, and learned, through challenging and meaningful activities, to become competent and confident contributors to the lives of their families. Children have not changed in their needs and ways of learning, but their environment has changed. The Children's Farm experience has shown us how well children respond to a setting that challenges them with real activities while allowing them to learn as children.

The hayloft offers important learning experiences for young children.

My proposal is not to build more barnyards where children can play and learn (although preserving this one for a school for young children has been a good use for an old dairy barn). Building barnyards for schools is not practical today. However, I challenge the reader to determine what it is about haylofts — Mrs. Linder saw it — that meets the needs of children and the way they learn best, and provide these elements through other, 'century appropriate' experiences.

I've observed children in that hayloft for years. To a child, the hayloft represents these learning experiences:

- First there's the clear and exciting physical challenge. "I am big, I can climb all the way up there myself. I was a little scared at first but now I wonder if I can jump all the way to the straw stack today."

- Along with the challenge comes the need to learn self-control. "I have to wait to get up here, but it's okay. There's not enough room for us all on the ladder. I can wait 'cause I like it so much up there."

- Listening skills are clearly needed. "I want to know what's going to happen and how to get up there. I'll listen."

- Understanding of the use of places is learned. "I'm helping up here; this place is cool!"

- In addition, using all the senses is an intriguing aesthetic experience. "It looks dark up here; hey, look! Shadows, lights on things, sparkles!"

- And it's something that can be done with others. "This is fun; we're all up here together!"

Schools can offer these experiences if they plan for them.

What can teachers and school planners do in today's schools and play yards to provide challenges for children, places where they can work together, learn bravery, and gain confidence? Certainly, by allowing enough time to play outdoors on physically challenging (while safe) playground equipment, including climbing and jumping. Social and emotional growth takes place as children meet challenges together, so some schools have begun to include playing with loose parts (boards and tree stumps), which we do as well. One of our popular outdoor areas includes a tire swing that allows for more than one child to swing together, and a zip line, appropriately positioned to challenge children as well as encourage courtesy: to wait their turn and to return the bar to the next child using it. A farm is not needed to have these opportunities for physical and social learning.

THOUGHTS FOR PARENTS

There are many ways parents can thoughtfully challenge their children.

A parent workshop I led searched for ideas of other 'haylofts' in kids' lives. They proposed riding a two-wheeler, tackling the monkey bars, or climbing the fireman's pole (the most difficult challenge for most school climbers). They discussed individual skills like ice skating, learning to swim, and jumping off the dock at Grandpa's cabin. These offered the exciting challenges and aesthetic joy, but perhaps did not include the shared adventure found in climbing a tree, hiking all the way around the pond with your family, or sledding down the 'big hill' with your best friend.

Several classic paintings show children at active, group games of physical play. Two of these often seen on the walls of our school are Breughel's *Children's Games* and Winslow Homer's *Crack the Whip*. Can jumping in the plastic balls at fast food restaurants or sliding down climbers in the play yards of standard daycare centers create the same interest and joy as seen on the faces of children in the past as they raced in the meadow or played around the neighborhood?

Search for a school that encourages active, hands-on learning as opposed to passive entertainment.

In looking for a school for your children, you may want to consider whether there are enough challenges — physical as well as mental — and whether the children are treated as competent, capable people as they learn together to rise to these challenges. While the mantra 'Learning Through Play' is certainly important for young children, for many schools and pre-planned curricula this doctrine has slipped into 'Learning Through Entertainment.' Children need active, hands-on involvement in doing real, meaningful activities that are challenging for them, with girls needing these opportunities as much as boys. The older days of 'sliding down the cellar door and climbing up that apple tree' do not exist for many children in North America, and so it has become important for homes and schools to provide them.

> *Say, say, say playmate, come out and play with me*
> *slide down my cellar door, climb up the apple tree ...*
> *and we'll be jolly friends, for ever more.*
> ~ old childhood rhyme

Ryan: "I'm just a little boy."

A young child shows us how he feels small
and how we can help him feel competent.

OCCASIONALLY, a child appears in our class who teaches us so much about other children. A few years back it was Ryan, a verbal, sensitive child who had the ability not only to say exactly what he was thinking, but also to let us know exactly how he was feeling at any time. Now, many children who are four-years-old may be verbal, but they are not all intimately in touch with their feelings. They know that they feel upset, but don't know why. We also see children who are intimately in touch with their feelings, but their feelings overwhelm them to the point that they cannot verbalize them. We see them crying, whining, or laughing, but not often describing their feelings.

But being with Ryan was like a having a window into his psyche. He told us how it felt to be small and afraid, he told us how he wanted to be big, and he told us how great he felt when he was competent. He taught us how all kids must feel!

Here was a typical scene with Ryan:

The children were climbing to the hayloft. Ryan stood in line at the bottom of the ladder, shoving his feet around in the hay, hands in his pockets, saying, to no one in particular, "I know I can do it, I've done it before, I'll do it real easy this time, I won't cry."

Then, as his turn arrived, his words changed. "I don't think I can do it," and "This is really hard," but he started on up. A teacher was close by, knowing what came next.

"I can't, I can't," he cried, hanging on the third rung with anguish written all over his face. We were right behind him, saying, "I'm sure you can. You did it before. There you go, only one more step …"

As he placed his trembling hand on the top rung, he'd say, "I'm little, this is hard," and then he'd shove his last foot over and say, "I'm up, I did it; it wasn't too hard!" and off he'd run to play.

This type of monologue continued throughout the year when he played with other children as well as when he tackled new physical challenges. Ryan's father was a policeman, a large, gentle man whom Ryan adored. However, Ryan also sensed, intensely, the vast difference in power and ability between his father and himself. His best way to approximate the power he wanted was to pretend.

Pretending is a healthy way for many children to feel powerful, but when Ryan pretended, he immersed himself in his play so wholeheartedly that the line between reality and imagination was blurred. Perhaps it is for many children. Ryan, being so emotional and so verbal, was able to show this to us.

Ryan usually arrived at school wearing one of his favorite outfits: a well-worn cowboy vest with a large pretend sheriff's badge pinned on it. One day he told us, "I'm big today 'cause I'm wearing my badge."

He loved leading the others in their imaginative play. He would pretend to be a grown-up, using a large, lower voice and say 'cop' things like, "I think the robbers are going around the other side … I'll go check it out." He usually played peacefully and creatively with the others, but one day Sammy had his own ideas, which he tried explaining to Ryan.

Ryan insisted it be his way. Soon we saw him tugging on an unwilling and protesting Sammy's arm. Coming over at first hint of a ruckus, a teacher said, "Hmm, it looks like Sammy has a different idea."

"But I'm a cop. I have to take him in. I have to arrest him. That's what cops do."

This time, as before, we explained to Ryan that cops help law-abiding people to be safe, but they don't get to boss them around. Here at school, we continued, Sammy gets to decide what he would do himself, just like Ryan gets to decide.

A minute later, though, another scuffle between Ryan and Sammy brought us quickly to the scene of the 'arrest,' where Ryan had punched Sammy. After soothing Sammy's feelings, we turned to Ryan, who was leaving the creative play area from which he had been temporarily banished. Ryan protested plaintively, "But I had to hit him. He's bigger than me." Under the sheriff's badge, after all, was a fearful little boy.

Our approach was to turn once again to the helpful tasks indoors, the Big Jobs outside, and the challenging physical activities that could teach Ryan, as no words from us could, how helpful, strong, and 'big' he really was learning to be. He gradually mastered the hayloft ladder without crying, remarking in May, "Remember when I was little and I used to cry?"

He learned to take turns and compromise with others, his sensitivity gradually expanding to include others' sensibilities as well as his own. He loved helping at cooking and proudly announced whenever he had helped with snack. "I cut those oranges," or "That cheese was really hard to spread." We were reminded how all the children probably felt this way, that Ryan articulated to us what they were all feeling.

In late spring, as we climbed over the big gate to go on a long hike, we were again reminded of this. Kids tumbled over quickly, unencumbered by those snowsuits of the last few months. Ryan, too, started eagerly over the gate, then, as if catching himself being competent, he stopped, and, passionately cried, "I can't, I can't do this! I'm just a little boy!"

"Sure you can," said his smiling teacher. "Just lift that strong leg up there, and your hand there," she pointed to the spot as we often did to encourage.

… "I'm just a little …" Ryan continued climbing, even while protesting … "I'm just … I'm … I'm BIG, I'm BIG!" He swung his leg over and started down the other side. "I did it, I'm BIG!"

And indeed he was as he ran, triumphantly, with dark eyes flashing and cheeks glowing, and caught up with big friends.

THOUGHTS FOR TEACHERS

Providing challenges can improve
a child's perception of himself and enhance learning.

How a child perceives himself drives much of that child's behavior. To help children see themselves as more competent and more successful, we plan and offer challenges for children. Researchers have remarked that people are at peak performance and most involved and motivated when the task is just a little bit harder than what they've accomplished in the past, but possibly within reach. The teacher's job becomes one of finding the right challenge for each child and providing the proper encouragement.

A 'challenge' is just a bit above
the child's current ability or perception.

At our school, a 'challenge' is a task that a child sees as difficult but is interesting, perhaps a little scary, and just hard enough to allow the child to attempt it. Because we are able to take the children outside frequently, many of our challenges are outdoors, as Ryan discovered. Climbing the ladder to our hayloft to play, climbing a big gate that leads to the pasture, sliding down the fireman's pole, or walking along an old fallen oak that has been converted to a safe but exciting climbing tree — these are included in our plans for the day, not so much as physical exercise, but as emotional development tools to help children approach challenges with confidence and begin to see themselves as competent.

Challenges can be included in the indoor program that are physical as well as social or intellectual in nature.

Some motivating challenges, however, present themselves indoors, especially in the useful and intriguing task of preparing food. Some challenges we plan for include: cracking an egg and beating it. (Do you know how scary it is to crack open an egg for the very first time?) Other challenges are cutting celery, carrots, or potatoes with 'real knives' (just table knives, but real, nonetheless); or flipping over pieces of French toast on a low, safely supervised griddle.

A playroom challenge might be a more complicated floor puzzle, a difficult building toy, a new game of cards or dominoes, or for those who are ready, the challenge of learning to write letters or numbers in meaningful context. The challenge for the teacher, and the most interesting one, is to know which child is ready for which challenge and to provide opportunities for children at all levels to find success.

The challenge of running

Another challenge we've seen children face at our school is simply 'running.' At many schools and homes children are often told, "Don't run, walk! You might fall. It might not be safe." Yet at the farm we see that children naturally want to run. Given enough space, most children will run, from one chore to another, from the climber to the garden, from the art project to the sandbox. The sheer joy of physical movement is a reality, yet I think the feeling of autonomy and freedom (*I can get there on my own!*) must be part of their desire to run as well.

A particular challenge at the beginning of the school year is running to the barnyard. It's a gravel drive and downhill. No one tells them to run; it seems they just want to. A few hardy children or returning children set the example, and soon the other "flatlanders" tiptoe down the slope, then go a little faster — gravity helps as they descend, — they go faster and faster! There are a few tumbles, but they learn to pick themselves up and try again, and within a few weeks everyone is doing it (unless they stop and smell the flowers or pet the cat on the way down).

THOUGHTS FOR PARENTS

There are many benefits to encouraging children to do things for themselves.

As Ryan showed us, children must feel small in a grown-up world. While adults attempt to make them feel safe and secure, it's good to be aware that anything we do for them is a reminder to them that we are bigger, stronger, and smarter. "I'm just a little boy," is often in the back of a young child's mind, probably explaining the desperation with which some of them fight to feel big, strong, and powerful any way they can. Parents can help them by remembering Rudolph Dreikurs' admonition: "Never do anything for a child which he can do for himself."

How to know when to make the 'parental shift.'

As children become more and more competent, parents can begin to shift from doing *for* to doing *with*, from helping by *doing for* to helping by *teaching how*. The more real challenges we can provide that helps children see themselves as competent, the more able they are to share, care, and follow rules when necessary. Encouraging our children to do such simple things around the home as hanging up his own coat or pouring her own juice does much to reinforce a child's perception that, "I'm big; I can try new things." For young children, perception of self is viewed from a physical standpoint, as in 'stuff I can do,' so being able to hang from the swing bar is much more intrinsically rewarding than being able to count to ten by rote. Praise does not have to, nor should it, enter in to the picture. The child is motivated by the challenge and by being able to meet it.

Here are some suggestions for ways to encourage young children at challenges.

And how to encourage? *Not* by talking too much about each thing a child does, but by encouraging where needed. Even if we think we're encouraging, sometimes our over-talking feels manipulative to a child. At the Children's Farm we like to use constructive commentary such as, "Looks like you're almost to the top now; your hands are holding strongly, now, the feet ..." instead of cajoling words like, "Come on, honey, you can do it, you can ..." Encouraging is real, cheerleading is unreal.

Because acceptance is important, we might comment, "Sometimes you feel a little scared," or "You decided not to jump from that bale today," so the child learns that doing a challenging thing is his idea and his feelings about it are legitimate. Remarks about effort, "You really pulled hard," and resilience, "Next time maybe you'll get all the way across," can keep children seeing themselves as able to rise to a future challenge.

Show your child that you believe he can do it; "Sure you can, just go on up." Give small pointers as she begins to slip; "Just a little stronger grip right here," and help the child learn to evaluate her progress. "It looks like you got a lot farther up than last time, doesn't it?" can be steps to confidence. Too much praise can backfire, as a child may wonder why we're so excited about such a little (now that he's done it) thing. Children know when they've reached the goal. A nod or smile from us is enough reward for them. Our own reward is that look in their eyes that says, "I've done it, I'm big."

Caitlin: "I can't."

As a child works with others, she realizes her capabilities.

OH, THERE GOES THAT WHINE AGAIN, I thought. This was going to be one of those needy days for Caitlin. I'd been hearing, "I can't, I can't." You help me." "Nancy, is this good?" "Sam, look at my picture." "Teacher, Teacher, help me get my mittens on," and on and on and on. I was running out of ways to help!

I was really surprised to hear it coming from Caitlin this year. She was tall, almost five, and as verbal and capable, both physically and cognitively, as any other child in this mixed age group of three- to five-year-olds. *Why does she continue to whine?* I asked myself.

At age three, Caitlin's verbal ability was an asset as she was quick to identify her wants and needs to her new teachers and classmates. She sang, listened to the stories, and followed the older children around, frequently whining to be let in on their play and often succeeding in being included. Her cheerful smile was frequent, but so was her occasional pout and frown, especially when confronted with any new challenge. Her teachers expected she would grow in confidence as she played and worked with the other children and that soon she would be able to negotiate in a conversational tone. Now in her second year at our school, while her legs and beautiful brown hair were both much longer, her whining vocabulary was larger, too. Caitlin was stuck, it seemed, at being three.

"Well, let's see, Caitlin, I think if you just grabbed on that side of your mitten, maybe ... ahh, yes, like that, you've got it." Just that little bit of attention was all she needed, but need it she did. Problem solved, we went outside to join the other children. A good inch of snow had fallen on the patio, and everyone was going out to help.

"I need a shovel, get me a shovel," whined Caitlin.

"Well, they're right there against the wall. You can pick one out for yourself," I answered cheerily, as if we hadn't mentioned to each and all that the shovels were waiting for them beside the door. I wondered, *are we encouraging or enabling her helplessness? What if I just let her stand there without a shovel; would she figure out how to get one?*

I remembered that Caitlin's family included two older brothers, who probably get Caitlin's shovel for her, or even more probably, do all the shoveling for her. *Hmm*. I may ask her mom if she's noticed this needy behavior at home. Surely they're all getting sick of this whining, too; I only hear it for two and a half hours!

I decided not to help Caitlin anymore that day if she could possibly help herself. There were a couple more whines ..."There's no room for me to shovel ... "

I continued working in a place where there was a lot of room. Caitlin began shoveling beside me, but soon was making longer and longer forays as she pushed the fluffy, sparkling snow aside to make paths in each direction.

"He threw snow in my face ... "

I glanced but thought it just a brief accident of white powder, and I kept shoveling. Caitlin became engaged in deciding whether to push the snow into the side mounds or lift it up and toss it. We shoveled on in silence.

I wish she could get out of her helpless role, I mused, and

find a way to be needed, rather than needy. We had tried pairing Caitlin with three-year-old Kelsey, but Kelsey also soon tired of the whining, and just did the jobs herself the best she could. Yet Caitlin could be such a great older friend for Kelsey: she has good pretend ideas, she likes to do puzzles, as does Kelsey. Caitlin just doesn't see how helpful she could be to Kelsey, I fretted. I would have gotten them shoveling together, but Kelsey wasn't at school yet.

"Cut that out, you shoveled my pile ..." I heard Caitlin pout to larger Kurt. Well, at least she didn't ask for my help there, I thought. Now if we could just work on 'cheery' ...

Wait, wasn't that Kelsey coming up the path? I turned and waved to Kelsey's mom to let her know we saw her child arriving late. Mom and I had a brief exchange about what must look like a real-life Brueghel painting: sixteen children bundled and swathed in mitts and scarfs and colorful snowsuits industriously using red shovels in contrast to the whiteness of the winter landscape.

It was not I who greeted Kelsey, but Caitlin, who saw Kelsey walking up the path, eyes agog as she viewed the busy 'shovelers.' She noticed that Kelsey didn't have a shovel, and fortunately, that I was busy talking to Kelsey's mom. So, without a word, she went to get the last waiting red shovel, walked down the path toward the watching Kelsey, and handed her the shovel. Together they pushed and scraped and cleared the path with the others.

Though Caitlin will probably never recall the day she got unstuck from being three, it was a memorable moment for me as her teacher. After that day, she began taking a helping role with Kelsey and she played confidently with the other children. Caitlin's whine gradually diminished as she found other ways to interact with teachers and children alike. Caitlin was on her way to being five!

THOUGHTS FOR TEACHERS

When given the opportunity, children will choose to be helpful.

At the Children's Farm we have what we call Big Jobs, tasks that several people can do together, that are useful and helpful, and ones for which the need or result is obvious to children. They often require physical exertion, problem solving and thinking, or language exchange (as in group planning or in giving or following directions.) Children are not required to do these jobs, but they usually come to them willingly. Like most people, they welcome the opportunity to be useful. If the job itself doesn't look inviting, stating a need — along with requesting help from the teachers or other kids — is *rarely* turned down.

An educational program can and should plan for Big Jobs on a regular basis.

These are not just accidental activities that kids do or teachers suggest, although a Big Job may arise at any time and teachers are always ready to respond, as with the snow shower. Most often teachers plan these jobs into the day and structure them into the classroom setup and outdoor planned environment. For instance, we have a fish tank, not just for children to learn about animals, but to create an opportunity for a Big Job when we change the water. Outdoors, our garden and yard are planned so that they allow much digging, raking, and sweeping. Child-sized but real tools are available for indoor and outdoor Big Jobs. In every daily schedule we try to include these things: something to do with others, something to do that is useful, and something to do for someone else. Often, a Big Job meets all these requirements.

Child psychologist Rudolph Dreikurs said, "Never do anything for a child that he can do for himself." In our school setting we have added the Big Job rule: *Never do any*

Big Job that could be done by children. This could mean something as simple as having the children help set up snacks or move a table, instead of doing it ahead of time. Mixing paint, sweeping up scattered sand from the sand table, and watering the plants are all possible Big Jobs in any classroom.

When teachers set up a new "pretend area," they also ask the children to help. Kids help gather all the tools and animals from the vet clinic and carry them to the storeroom, and then, depending on class and tasks at hand, are often seen working together to carry the post office desk and boxes of letters and stamps back to the school room to set up the new post office area. After helping create the play area, they are more likely to engage with their friends at playing together there.

Outdoors, it means we save some of the shoveling or raking for the children to do. Those living in snowy climates can testify to the snow shoveling and sweeping opportunities, as well as our famous spring melt, in which our children scrape small drainage channels to eliminate the water buildup in our school parking lot. Hydrodynamics study and scientific inquiry? Certainly, but the pride and look of accomplishment we see on their faces testify to the emotional benefits of being useful, helpful, and competent.

Mixed-age groups facilitate both competency skills and social learning.

Having children of different ages together in the same classroom benefits both the younger and the older child, allowing older children to learn to help others, and giving younger children the opportunity to learn social skills and strive to attain the language and physical skills of those a bit older. Teachers can encourage these interactions; the Caitlin/Kelsey match-up continued to be a helpful social, emotional, and cognitive situation for both children for the remainder of that school year.

THOUGHTS FOR PARENTS

Modern lives offer fewer ways for children to have a role in the family.

Even as infant studies in child development laboratories across the country testify to the drive of children to be effective and to affect their environment, even as child psychologists agree about the need of children — and of all people — to feel competent and contributing, we in the United States are increasingly raising a generation of children who have nothing to do. Parents today may provide love, screen time, and toys galore, but few opportunities for helping, thereby neglecting a child's need to feel useful and competent.

If children do not have their competency needs met, they will find other ways to achieve power.

Feeling powerless, children turn to whatever they can in order to have some control over their surroundings. As Dreikurs observed, for some, their pattern of behaving becomes manipulative; asking for help becomes a way of controlling those who care for them. For others it becomes confrontational, demanding to have their way in a world where there seems no other way for them to be. Others may simply give up, passively letting their environments shape who they become and what they do, and missing possibilities and potentials to become truly capable and contributing members of society. What's a parent to do?

Parents can make a conscious effort to create positive roles for our children in the family.

Starting early, we *can* find ways for children to take part in the daily life of the home, not just by asking them their opinions, but by asking for their help. Remember the rule of thumb — *don't do anything a child could do.* Children can help sweep, sponge the tables (fun, even for a two-year-old!) and put their dishes in the sink. It may mean adjusting equipment, like providing step stools for kids to reach the sink, or lower pegs for them to hang their clothes. It could mean planning a small garden, getting a pet, or creating a family project with the idea of providing a means for creating Big Jobs. It means believing that our children can be competent; can setting the washer and dryer be harder than those iPads they conquer so easily? It does mean giving up our own need as parents to do things *for* our children. Remember that one of the most important gifts we can give children is teaching them how to do something. It's a gift that lasts forever.

Continued observation and reevaluation of our children and their self-perceptions can be important.

While it has been said that an important part of teaching is observation, the same can be proposed of parenting. When is our child's whine an expression of her need to have a more functional role in the family? When can asking an older child to help a younger one be of use to both children, or when can it be too much power for the older child and too disabling for the younger child? When are we limiting our children by being 'stuck' in their being a certain age? Thoughtful observation and consideration of our children's growing abilities as well as being aware of the need of all people to be challenged and useful can be our guidelines as we provide a family setting in which all can grow.

Bianca: "Look what we found."

A birthday girl feels lost without her best friend,
until a shared task gives her confidence to make new friends.

IT WAS AN EARLY SPRING DAY and the children were playing indoors, but Bianca, long-legged and bright-eyed, was wandering about the room. She had reached five-years-old that day, and a large paper was spread on the floor for the children to sign and draw pictures as a birthday card for her. Children took a break from playing in the space ship, tracing rocket pictures, looking at books, and playing in the sand table, to write a 'note' on Bianca's card. But Bianca couldn't settle in to play, for she missed her friend, Hannah.

Her frequent and favorite playmate had been asked to go outside with another group to do some chores and play together. The teachers occasionally divided the large group into smaller ones, especially on days like that one when a new, exciting space play station made its first day appearance. Smaller groups assure that all get a chance to participate. Inside, Bianca walked from art table to puzzles and back to the book corner, looking, but not choosing anything. Was Bianca wondering whether she could manage without her friend? Were old habits making her feel younger on this day, a day she was supposed to be 'turning older?'

Nathan, a confident five-year-old, had no problems missing his usual playmates, who were also in the outside group. He busily messed around in the sand table and soon proposed his own Big Job to the teacher. "There's lots of sand here on the floor," he announced in an authoritative voice. "I think I should clean it up!" He went to get one of the child-sized brooms hanging by the sink.

"Good idea," said Jenny, the teacher. As Bianca strolled by, Jenny saw a chance to involve a second person. "It looks like this is a Big Job ... maybe you could help Nathan?" Bianca, somewhat grudgingly, agreed.

Sand is actually fun to sweep, and soon the children were joined by Carter. Three brooms pushed the sand together in two piles. It was then that I, the school director, walked past. "Ah, this looks like a really Big Job." Nods from the children. "What will you do with these piles?"

Uncertain looks ... sweeping was what it had been about. "Well, let's see," I asked, "Do you think this is clean sand or dirty sand?"

"Dirty," claimed Bianca, and the two boys nodded in agreement, sweeping the piles into the dust pan as I held it.

"Well, then, we'd better not put it back in the sand box. Hmm ..." (pause, looking at the kids), "I know, you could take it outside!"

"Good idea, Nancy," said Bianca, her voice warm with approval, as if she were the teacher and I, Nancy, the child! Bianca held out her hands to take the dustpan.

Nathan opened the door while Bianca tiptoed out on the patio, sock-footed, to dump the sand six feet away in the iris bed. Going on about my business just inside the office door, I noticed that the three children continued to sweep and dump, sweep and dump, each taking turns and talking about who should hold the pan, who should open the door, etc. Then I heard hushed, excited ... "Bring it in, Bianca!"

Bianca entered proudly, holding a round, fist-sized rock with speckles on it, just about the size of a ... a ... a ... dinosaur egg? "Look what we found!" She reverently placed it on the science table, where she was joined by Nathan and Carter. They all whispered speculatively about the properties of the golden egg and took turns examining it with hand-held magnifying glasses. A wonder of nature, a rock previously buried under the piles of dirty snow, had been discovered by the three new friends.

THOUGHTS FOR TEACHERS

Flexible, changing small groups help children learn with a variety of different people.

The children in this story have had much experience with Big Jobs. Notice that Nathan actually created one for himself. The job of the adults here is to encourage and validate. Observing that Bianca needed to be involved with others, the teacher suggested the joint effort. Again, children rarely say 'no' to a true request for assistance. Once Bianca joined in the mutual effort, conversation flowed, camaraderie followed; can learning be far behind? Children who have confidence in their own ideas, as well as their own abilities, approach learning new things with that same confidence. Curiosity flourishes in the shared wonder. Where did the learning begin here? Let's just say that working together makes the learning together come more easily.

Working together on Big Jobs can lead to other kinds of learning, both social and intellectual.

Humans are social animals, and learning takes place in a social environment, as Bandura and other psychologists have been researching for years. The ability to work and learn comfortably with a variety of people is important as children approach the formal school years. At our school, we occasionally assign children to flexible and changing groups as a means of encouraging children to participate with an ever-widening circle of friends. Necessary at times in order to have a better experience at a Big Job, or to allow more to participate in a new pretend play area, smaller groups can allow conversation and interaction with different people and give social confidence to children as they find success.

THOUGHTS FOR PARENTS

Children have different understandings of what it means to be a friend.

Every parent wants his or her child to have friends. But what do we mean when we speak of friends for preschool-aged children? Parents may ask, "Do you have a friend at school?" To young children, a friend is someone who likes to play at what you like to play, a friend is someone you admire, or a friend is someone who helps you. Naming friends as if they are possessions can cause children to see people in that light: mine, yours, like me, not like me, do what I say, don't do what I say. Mistaken beliefs in what is expected of them can lead to jealousy, over-possessiveness, and that 'weapon' of the play yard: "You can't come to my party, you're not my friend."

We like to stress the importance of 'being' a friend, not 'having' one.

If our child frequently asks to play with the same child, perhaps it's time to invite some new children over, to keep the flexibility and social learning flourishing. No, our child doesn't 'need' a certain friend to be with, she needs to learn she can make and be a friend with many different children.

Birthdays can be overdone and cause stress for young children.

Birthdays are special days. Parents especially like them because, of course, it is an important milestone for them. In a child's life, every day is a milestone, a step up and forward, certainly in growing, hopefully in learning. At school we sometimes see the results of birthdays gone awry, when the tension and expectations built up in the child awaiting a birthday far exceed the celebration of the day. Yes, some friends over, the family gathered 'round, a time for congratulations and reminiscence, but too much effort put into creating the perfect and most spectacular birthday party for young children can misfire. At our school we sometimes find that we need to actively *downplay* a child's 'special' day. We provide a card for classmates to sign, we sing Happy Birthday, and all join in congratulating by 'clap/counting' the years the child has achieved. Otherwise we plan a normal day for that child, hoping that learning and growth can continue even — and often in spite of — this being a birthday.

Anna: "You're gonna love this!"

*A child gains confidence with encouragement
from observant and sensitive teachers.*

ANNA'S GREAT DAY had actually begun poorly. She and her mother got out of her car in the parking lot, carrying two dolls, a small doll blanket and a doll's bottle. It looked like a crisis of confidence was brewing. Mom looked inquisitively at me, the teacher. "I was telling Anna these babies should stay in the car?" she asked, as if appealing for agreement.

"Oh, my, yes," I'd replied. "We're planning a big outdoor day and they would get dirty. You'd need to set them down to feed the animals and ride the pony." On a sunny fall day at our school, children and parents know the routine. Chores, then play, hikes and pony rides are common nice day activities.

Anna tossed her head, frowning toward her mom, ready to take a stand she might regret. "Here's the deal, Anna," I stooped down and said firmly but kindly (I hoped), "We like you to keep your own toys for your house, and play with the different things that are here. That's the way it is!"

Mom took the dolls. Hopefully, she understood, if Anna didn't. After two more goodbye kisses, she still clung persistently to her mother's legs. I was surprised, because in the three weeks since school began this fall, Anna had been an enthusiastic participant and separation had not been an issue as far as we had seen. I was confident she could have a successful two and one-half hours without dolls or Mom.

I caught her mother's eye. She was gently pushing Anna toward me, trying to disengage from her arms. "Would you like me to help Anna wave goodbye to you?"

"Yes," said a relieved mom. I bent down beside Anna, giving her a hug while her mother peeled herself off and got in her car and drove away, waving and smiling, trying to exude confidence herself, pretending she didn't see the tears or hear the wails.

"I know, I know. Sometimes it's hard to say goodbye," I said, gently patting Anna on the back. We turned together to see what the others were talking about. Soon, despite a lingering tear on her still rosy cheek, Anna was listening to another child tell my co-teacher, Mary, of her upcoming trip. Another minute and Anna was adding that soon she would be going to Disneyland to ride in a big red boat. I smiled at the quick recovery.

Once all were counted and the day's plan discussed, Anna hurried with her class to the black-topped play area. There she ground corn, played with corn kernels in the sensory table, painted a picture on an outdoor easel, and held the baby kittens. When it was her turn to ride the pony, she came into the pen confidently, wearing today, as she often did, her pink riding boots with the fringe on the top. A tall and sturdy girl for her age, Anna was a competent rider. She climbed on, started, stopped, and steered the pony, needing little assistance as she rode with the teacher walking beside her. She gave Rosie a big hug on the muzzle after she slid to the ground.

Soon it was time for snacks. Children washed hands and gathered together around our large picnic blanket to sing a few songs. As the designated song leader, I chose carefully. It was early in the year, and I didn't want to make group time too long, I silently reminded myself. Just one fun activity song about our pony ride, where the children held pretend reins, pulled back to pretend stop, and patted their legs to sound like horses walking and trotting. Then I'd try one new song about a squirrel, just a short one.

As the horse song ended, Anna blurted out … "I know a good song," before I could begin the squirrel.

"What is it?" I wanted to encourage her eager contribution, considering her shaky start this morning.

"Oh, it's a great song! It's about a horse, too."

She paused, looking around at all the children in the circle, "Oh, you are all gonna love this," she said. "I'll sing it. BUT," she added, raising her voice, "It takes A LOT of patience to hear this, but you'll love it." She looked around again at all their faces.

She began singing, "I have a little pony, and she stays in her pen and my little pony is nice …" or something like that.

"BUT THEN," she interrupted her own singing, hands in the air as she looked around the circle again. The children were mesmerized; all eyes were on Anna. "Can you make that horse walking sound?" she asked them.

Who could refuse? All began to 'walk' the horse on their legs. "Now the horse gets out of her pen. She goes over to the pigs. Who can make the sound of the pig?"

"Snort, snort, snort," went all the children.

"BUT WAIT!" Anna stopped them with a wave of her hand. "I think I hear the horses." A sweeping glance, "Who can make the horse sound?"

"Neigh, whinny," from all of us.

I glanced at my co-teacher, Mary. *Yes, let her continue, this is great and they're all with her on it*, we communicated silently.

"The horse visits the ducks; can you do the duck sound?"

"Quack, quack, quack," echoed all the children.

"BUT …" (by raising her voice and her hands she eloquently stopped the ducks while she continued the horse's travels to the accompaniment of the children's hands. "Now he walks ve-ry slow-ly. Now he runs…"

"Pat, pat, pitter, pitter pat," from all the children's hands on their laps.

How could she do this? I was thinking. Our third week of school! I don't know if I could hold their attention that long with a giant picture book, let alone a story. Another glance at Mary … *Let her go on*, we silently agreed, and the story continued.

After a few more animal visits, with accompanying sounds, the tale bogged down a bit, something about a bad man who wanted to kill the horse. I intervened. "This is pretty long and we're getting hungry. Does anyone want to eat?" I proposed.

"Yes, no," everyone voiced an idea. "Let's vote," suggested teacher Mary. A short vote revealed that all children wanted to eat and all wanted to continue the story. (Four-year-olds don't get it about not voting twice, we should have known!)

We passed out the crackers and cheese. Anna cheerfully ate with the rest. I wondered, should we just go on with the day? But, no, we had voted … I wanted to respect their choices, didn't I?

"So, Anna … how did that story end?"

"The horse ran" … turning to the other kids … "Let's all make that horse run …"

"Pitter, patter, pitter," went their ready hands.

"And it went to its pen and it went to sleep. Now pretend to sleep," she cued in the eager actors who were quickly tucking their heads on their hands, nap style.

"What a great ending!" I interjected, shamelessly praising

and sincerely admiring, and we all clapped. "Thank you, Anna!"

Anna was clearly pleased with herself. Her teachers were pleased, too, and not just with her, but with all the children. They had listened so well, and we all knew we were a group. The kind of feeling teachers plan to develop, that togetherness that we strive to make happen, and here we had a four-year-old do it for us!

The day hadn't begun well for Anna, but at morning's end she went out to her waiting car with a feeling of accomplishment and of being appreciated in a real way, not for her dolls, but for her gift of a story that we were all privileged to receive.

Social/Emotional Development

THOUGHTS FOR TEACHERS

Stick to your rules,
when you know why you have them.

We know from experience that these toys brought from home may begin as a security blanket, but often become a hindrance rather than a help to children at our half-day school. They fret about them instead of interacting with other children or engaging in the various and changing school activities. In addition, for some they become a status symbol, a way to "bribe" friends, as in "I'll let you hold my doll if you'll be my friend," or worse, to exclude certain children as in "No, you can't play with her, only my best friend can play with her." We know that if we give in one day and a child brings a special toy, the next day three or four other children will be bringing their possessions to bribe, manipulate, or defend their friendships.

Of course, that is not what this school is all about. Most of the children here have ample toys at home, perhaps too many. They need lessons in the sharing of non-owned toys and tools, or better yet, ideas, as opposed to their own status-laden accouterments from home. It would have been easy to give in and allow her to bring her dolls, one more time. Aside from the 'possessions' issue, we wonder what else she wouldn't have done that day, if she had been fussing over those dolls, as she had the time before. What a loss that would have been!

Observation is key.

Watch and observe children to see how they are feeling. Emotionally, we could see Anna recovered quickly, yet we also continued to build on her feelings of competency with her chores, her pony ride, so that by singing time, she was ready to contribute, big time!

Be ready to change plans to promote optimal learning.

Along with observation comes the flexibility to build on the experiences of the day and be able to change daily plans. What if we had said, "I'm sorry, we don't have time for your song now, Anna; it's time to eat"? Of course, sometimes we do have to say that, yet Anna's story taught us the value of flexibility once again.

Every class is different.

Along with flexibility to meet the needs of individual children comes flexibility to meet the needs of different classes. A class might have been too wiggly to make it through a second song, or we could have decided to end an activity sooner because it looked like it was going to rain and we'd need to start inside. Teachers with outdoor curriculums and classrooms learn the necessity of weather flexibility, but differences between classes can also cause teachers to change the plans. Perhaps taking a hike together first if children are needing to run, or not taking a planned hike because someone was feeling very sad about missing Mom. Observation and communication are indeed "key."

THOUGHTS FOR PARENTS

At separation time, remember what a child gains at school.

It's hard to leave a crying child at school. We feel mean and non-caring. We may have things planned, or work to do, so we may start to feel guilty. Or we see the tear-stained face and remember that baby of just a few months ago. Here's when it's good to keep our rationality above our emotions and remember why we had decided our child was ready for school or daycare, and what we thought was good about it for her. She doesn't know that at this tearful moment, but her parent does!!

Show children by our actions that we believe in their abilities.

When our child was a baby she needed us; now she needs us to believe in her. Courage is learned gradually and the greatest gift we can give our child is our confidence in her. This child has a lot of strengths she can draw on and she needs to learn, in a gentle and gradual way, how to discover those strengths. As we leave our 'Anna,' remember what a strong and talented child she is, as Anna's mother did. We can be confident that the teachers and caregivers we've chosen will appreciate her talents.

Part 2: Foundations of Learning

Jennifer: "I know that day!"

A child's remark inspires some observations
on the connections between experience and words.

"I KNOW THAT DAY!" I still get a thrill when I recall Jennifer's breathless words that day over twenty years ago. For me it was the day I thought I'd first observed the power of literature with young children.

It was a story about a heron that walked slowly through a pond, past lots of wildlife hiding from it. The book, filled with beautiful pictures, began with the lyrical, descriptive words. "The sun shone, glistening, on the water."

I read softly and with a whisper of wonder, hoping to pull in the wigglers and jigglers with my tone of voice. I paused to turn the page and heard Jennifer, with blue eyes wide and mouth open in excitement, gasp and blurt out, "Ah ... I KNOW that day!"

It was a goose-bump moment for me. As I continued the story, I could tell that all the children were with me straight through to the end. "The silent pond awaited as the bees buzzed and the water sparkled." Jennifer was right, I thought, they all 'knew that day.' What a story! What a testimony to the power of literature! To write something where a reader can say, "I know that day," why, that's what good writing is all about. This is why we read to children, so they can know that day!

Many children, pond visits, and nature books later, I now see that still memorable day differently. Gradually, over the years of teaching and observing, I came to believe it was not the literature that made the experience at the pond come alive, but instead, the previous experience this child had had which made the literature come alive. And that insight has become the guideline for our sharing of literature at the Children's Farm — the experience comes first, and then the book.

Of course Jennifer knew 'that day.' I remember what her prior experiences had been that year. I can still see Jennifer and her classmates scuffling out to the pond on a blustery March day. "Where has all the ice gone?" they debated, as they kicked at stones and sticks along the edge. They gathered around, round eyed, as their teacher pointed out the raccoon footprints in the mud.

I saw Jennifer a week later looking for the first little bits of green in nettle sprouts and bramble buds as she and her classmates searched for the first "clues" of spring's arrival. The warm sun washed her face as all turned to feel its glow. Surely, spring would come soon, they faithfully agreed.

Then I saw Jennifer with her mittens back on again; the air felt like winter, but something was astir. The teachers were promising a surprise down at the pond. We must tiptoe slowly, they admonished, and not make a sound. Instead we pantomimed. *Stop, do you hear? What, What? Do you hear? Yes, yes* ... they all heard as they gained the shelter of the pine trees at the edge of the pond. The spring peepers' ebullient chirping was earsplitting as the children approached. Soon they forgot to tiptoe and began chirping and chattering excitedly among themselves. As the children's volume rose, the frog chirps subsided, then, "wait ... oh, they're gone." Quiet again, the children sat quivering and listening. They stood as still as four-year-olds possibly could. And yes, there came the chirps! One by one the peepers joined in again until the peeper chorus filled the air once more.

I saw Jennifer later that day, sitting on a rug in the schoolroom with her classmates. They nibbled on popcorn before a chart as each child helped add ideas to a class list of signs of spring: "How we know Spring Is Coming." Each had an idea; they tried as hard as they could to hold it in their minds as they waited their turn to say, "We saw green buds," or "The sun was warmer," or "The spring peepers were out." After hearing a list of their own ideas read back to them, the children joined in a chorus or two of "Five Green and Speckled Frogs," counting fingers aloft as they joyfully jumped their frog fingers into the pond.

And so, on the day of Jennifer's insightful response to literature, hopefully all the children in her class knew that day. The words read from a piece of paper, so descriptive and clear, became a memory, a symbol, and a mental image, not seen by any one child, but shared by all through the wonder of the written word.

THOUGHTS FOR TEACHERS

Children learn best by direct experience.

Piaget, developmental psychologists, cognitive scholars, all tell us that young children are in an experiential, doing and manipulating stage. Teachers know this, and yet so often we offer them second-hand experiences, 'hands on' with copies of things, words instead of doing. Well, yes, we do want to help them learn to make that connection between their experiences and the written word, but we will be more effective if we start first with the *doing.*

After children have manipulated, acted on, experimented with, and created using real things, we then begin making the link to learning through symbolic thought and symbols. After offering them interesting and motivating activities with real things, we move into the recalling stage, talking with children about what they have learned, helping them to symbolize their learning.

Build on experiences using planned art, song, and conversational activities.

Some art projects are 'memory pictures' and we call them that for children: the gluing of eggs and feathers after they have petted chicks and washed and cooked eggs; the bouquet made from dried weeds and grasses found on a walk and saved in a cup of plaster of Paris; the painting with blue and white paint after playing in the blue and white powder snow of winter. These 'memory pictures' are the first symbols of children's real-life experiences, and the first glimpses of what the world of art can mean for them.

Music memories: songs about sledding, about frogs (peep, peep), about chickens (cluck, cluck), all teach children the power of music to evoke and reminisce. Experiences that were exciting and motivating at the time become wonderful to sing about together in remembrance.

Simple conversations shared around a snack or after a song, 'what we did today,' 'what we liked best,' or 'where we went' can help children solidify their memories and reinforce their vocabularies about what they learned or did.

Gradually begin working written symbols into real activities.

After recalling, teachers can expand the children's experiences by introducing plans and projects, using functional language and numbers as ways to make these real projects work. A chart of birds seen, a list of ideas about spring coming, a sign showing what kinds of seeds were planted, a list of names of the kittens, a group story about our hike to listen to the peepers: these are all ideas of teacher-planned use of written symbols springing from experience.

Everyday reading is important to make the link.

While building on real experiences shared at our school, such as animals, nature, or real activities, we choose books from many cultures worldwide that show some shared universal feelings, even though the faces and places may be different. Our goal is to teach the value, wonder, and beauty of literature, to make children aware of that connection between the written symbol and very real thoughts, ideas, and experiences. But *read it last*.

THOUGHTS FOR PARENTS

Do it first.

Educators and parenting experts cite the studies showing that children whose parents read to them have more success in school. I'm convinced it is not simply the book, but it's also the language, the time together, and the shared ideas as we read with our child that make the difference in later reading ability and interest.

Think of these important things that reading offers and see how other things can also give these kinds of experiences. Then, one night a week, instead of reading a story, we could step outside and count the stars together. Another evening, perhaps, read a recipe, make the cookies, and share them with people we love. Or write a letter to Grandma, telling her about all the new green things in the back yard. While driving in the car, instead of listening to another CD (iTunes?), we can make up a song together about what it feels like to go sledding, swimming, or playing at the playground (something active that our child has done).

We can share books that link meaning to words.

When choosing stories for preschoolers, we can find ones with a familiar theme or point of reference but stretch from there. Or we can plan experiences to make our book choice most salient. Want to read an old favorite, *The Little Engine That Could?* Great literature, but for even greater impact, we can dig out those old toy trains for a couple of days, stop at the nearest train track and get out to hear and feel one rumble by, work together pulling sleds up the hill by huffing and puffing, and then read those wonderful words while snuggling together at bedtime. Now it's easier to understand the rhythm and meaning of 'I think I can, I think I can.' Through the magic of literature, they can "know that day."

Devin: "There's my idea!"

*A child's solution to a problem in a storybook
creates an exciting and original group story.*

"THEY SHOULDA JUST DUG IT UP!" mumbled five-year-old Devin as the children filed out of the playroom where they had been listening to a favorite story. This day we had decided to read the old Russian tale *The Turnip* by Janina Domanska with the idea that perhaps one of the groups would enjoy acting it out on a later date. The children sat engrossed in the story of the farmer and his wife and all their animals trying to pull a huge turnip out of the ground. Then Devin's comment, a logical one, caught the ears of the teacher closing up the book. It was the end of the day, no time to pause, but the next class day, instead of acting out the story book, the teachers acted upon Devin's reaction.

"What's your idea?" we asked. "How else could the farmer get the turnip out?"

On a large piece of paper, we drew a turnip half way out of the ground, writing the words at the top of the page: HOW TO GET A HUGE TURNIP OUT OF THE GROUND.

We had accomplished group stories with the children before; sometimes a bit of prodding and coaxing was needed to inspire all to contribute. This time, however, a jumble of ideas rushed forth, one after the other, quickly, building on earlier ideas.

"Pound it with a hammer." said one. The teacher quickly wrote the words down, followed by that child's name, as the next idea tumbled out.

"Dig a hole with a shovel."

"Or," added another, "you could use your hand ... just push it up." The teacher was scribbling fast now!

"I know ... dig a big hole and get a dump truck. Put the dirt in the dump truck," exclaimed a frequent truck player, and his idea soon appeared in print before him.

"I'd dump it in a big pile like where they're building a new house." said the foremost block builder of the class. "Use a rope around the bottom and pull!" shouted out an eager outdoor player.

And so it continued. We had to ask them to slow down so one teacher could write all the ideas on the paper. The session continued for a good ten minutes, after which we read over the list of ideas to the group. Now most everyone listened intently, waiting for each idea to be read, but interested in other solutions as well!

"Use a chain saw and cut off the root."

"Or use a saw, scooping it out."

"One of those things that wrecks walls ... a wrecking ball."

"A big kind of truck that has a seat on the top and a seat on the bottom."

"A garbage truck. Scooping it up like tiger claws."

As even more ideas were proposed, we suggested that people could come over during free play time and offer another idea for the teacher to document. While other children played, we also made a point of asking some of the quieter members of the class for their contributions. We know that some children have good ideas, but prefer not to talk in large groups, so telling it later to a teacher is always an option for our group stories.

"Get a big dinosaur and let him get it."

"Use a big old digger. It has spikes on the end."

"Get a big rock under it and push it out."

"Dig it out with a shovel."

"Use a drill. Drill a hole in it. A really big one and it scoops it out."

"A big hammer that breaks up the streets. A sledge hammer."

"Take a saw and cut off the top of the turnip."

"A sled and put it on it. But the sled would be broke. Get a wagon."

"Leave it in the ground forever."

These results greatly exceeded even Children's Farm teachers' optimistic expectations of the capabilities of young children. They testify to the ingenuity and problem-solving abilities of the three-, four- and five-year-olds involved. We kept the Idea List posted in the classroom for several days, and even added a few sketches. Children frequently came over and pointed to a line, saying, "There's my idea!"

THOUGHTS FOR TEACHERS

Solicit children's ideas in problem solving or purposeful group stories.

In a 1994 issue of Young Children, Lillian Katz, president of the National Association for the Education of Young Children, proposed that teachers rethink the use of group stories or lists which have the purpose of promoting self-esteem. She was referring to those lists that go: 'I like this,' or 'I have that,' and she wondered if this exercise promoted narcissism rather than true self-esteem. She suggested that teachers find subjects on which children can ponder, problem solve, and wonder together.

We try hard to create stories that challenge thinking and generate ideas.

Intrigued by the challenge, our teachers have since made a greater effort to create group stories that demanded ideas about problems, called forth descriptions or events, or included instructions about what to do. Included have been 'how-to' lists (How to Go Sledding), newsletters for home (A Baby Lamb Was Born Today) and letters (Thank you for selling us the pony; he's doing fine, we like him because ...) These have almost completely replaced the lists of 'What I did today' and 'What I like.' We have also extended this more complicated use of language to express ideas in the words children ask us to write under their individual drawings. ("This is my brother. He is crying because he has a sore tooth and I am trying to cheer him up.")

More than self-esteem, it also becomes an exercise in mutual respect.

While teachers often see group story reading as a pre-reading activity and writing group stories a pre-writing adventure (an adventure because you never know what they are going to say), at the Children's Farm the writing of group stories is indeed an exercise in mutual respect and self-esteem. Each child is encouraged to remember, to voice, and to recall ... "there's my idea!"

In addition to reinforcing the validity of real ideas, we see group stories helping children see that their thoughts are equally valid and important. All ideas are written down, taking some agility on the part of the teacher in order to keep the ideas coming and somewhat to the point of the discussion as well. We've polished up some useful phrases like "Can you hold that thought?" and "We'll hear your idea next as soon as we write down Timmy's," and finally, "Let's read all the ideas we've got so far, in case someone else wants to add a new thought." These words assure children that we believe they are all capable of contributing intellectually, as we work to include them all in a more-or-less spontaneous format.

The use and need for language and symbols becomes more meaningful.

A valuable byproduct to the goal of promoting true self-confidence and respect for the ideas of others is that since the subjects are more interesting and children are more involved, the pre-reading and pre-writing message of communicating by the written symbol becomes not only much more salient to children, but a much more desired skill. "How do you write dragon?" they ask as they scribble on their circle with the tail.

THOUGHTS FOR PARENTS

Parents can reinforce the use of language for thinking.

Language development is important for young children, and parents are uniquely suited to teach early language development. We love every gurgle and squeak our babies make, and we glory in the new nouns they learn as we do in their naming of colors and numbers. Yet we often stop there, and threes and fours may continue in seeing language as something to use to get what they want or to gain control. ("I want a ..." and "get me a ..." being about where many of them seem to be when they arrive at group settings) rather than as a tool for expressing and sharing ideas. We can expand and develop children's language and thinking if we thoughtfully work at getting past the *naming* and *asking* stage into the *describing with wonder*, *proposing a hypothesis* and *having an idea* stages.

Help children learn to talk about ideas:

*Asking children what they think as many times as we ask them what they want.

*Asking questions that prompt new ideas, as in "Do you suppose it lives in that hole?"

*Wondering with kids. "I wonder why that dog barked at us?"

*Adding words like "problem, figure out, think, idea, guess, wonder and discover" to our discussions with children.

*Resisting the temptation to know all and explain all to children. Asking them their ideas or giving a little information at a time: "One thing I know is that ..." and seeing where the information takes them in their thinking.

*Reading a story to preschoolers and asking how the story might end differently, such as, "what would happen if ...?"

* Making up new stories together.

**Positive self-esteem can grow
from having a good idea and sharing it.**

Children have intelligent brains. We don't need to teach them to think, but we can challenge them to think with more complexity, and teach them how to share their thinking, name their ideas, and organize their thoughts through the use of language. It's a wonderful task. And self-esteem flourishes in a valid way when children feel confident and competent at sharing their thoughts. To us, an even more exciting experience than hearing those first gurgles and squeaks can be when we first hear our child say, "Here's my idea …"

Nick: "Would ya look at that!"

An adult-oriented child learns to interact with his peers during group conversation time.

WHAT A CURIOUS CHILD, and such a delight to have in a group! These were my first impressions of Nick. He gazed with great interest at the teachers, blond curly head turned to face them. He'd nod and watch intently as directions were given for the plan of the day, or as the story was read after snack. I can see him watching me, with bright grey-blue eyes as I tried to get the attention of his classmates, wiggly first-timers, three- and four-year-olds, to hear the words of an adult addressing a group (as if they even knew what a group was!) Nick certainly set a good example for attentiveness, I thought.

Nick, a child raised largely by his adoring grandparents, would frequently include the phrases of an older generation in his chirping speech patterns: "Say ... would ya look at that ..." as he'd point toward the cheeping bird or blossoming flower, looking up at the teacher as if sharing a special moment with them. And that was precisely the problem for Nick. While we recognized that his verbal skills and inquisitiveness were wonderful assets, we were finding that Nick was using them to gain attention — attention from the adults.

Here's what we were seeing. We were on our way out to the pasture, proceeding to the big oak trees that would be our first "waiting place." Some children raced down the hill, or rolled tumbling past each other on the crisp, dry grass of fall, others ambled hand and hand with a friend. Nick walked beside me, the teacher, chattering and commenting in his usual ways ... "What is this, where are we going? Why is this so sticky and pokey? What is that?"

Instead of answering each and every question, I directed his attention toward the object of interest — the plant, the cow pie — with, "What do you think?" or "It's so interesting; what do you think it looks like?" I countered. And I would turn his comment toward the others. "Maybe one of the other kids know where we're heading, you could ask someone, maybe Keisha or James if you're not sure ..." To no avail, they had all skipped ahead and were waiting eagerly by the oak tree to learn of our next waiting place. We teachers had determined ahead of time that we would walk over the hill and "accidentally" discover the giant bleached-out bones of the long-departed bull that we knew were there, but that this class had not yet seen.

Then, leading the group through the tall grass, I saw that Nick was still glued beside me, wanting, needing, to be with an adult. As we arrived at the bones, I was amused to hear, once again, his grandfatherly phrase, "Well ... would you look at this!" but wished, once again, that he could share this observation with all of us, not just me, the attendant adult of the group. Still, his comment did help get the others to rally around the discovery. I thought, odd, how for some of the others I wish the focus of Nick, while for Nick I wish the ability to relate to others. Well, they're all different (a common muse).

"Do you think it's a dinosaur? Is this the leg? Can I hold that one?"

"Maybe Johnny has an idea about what it is. You could ask him ..." I persevered, but no, it was still the adult he wanted, needed ...

As winter approached, the class began spending more time indoors. While he liked the art projects and the cooking jobs, pretend play was daunting for Nick, because it meant interacting and sharing ideas with other children. He was good at ideas and at talking, but only if we adults played there with him. We continued to hope that soon he would learn that his ideas needed no outside validation, and furthermore, that other kids had interesting ideas, too.

Appropriately enough, it was during Conversation Time that talkative Nick discovered both himself and other kids. By this time, we'd moved indoors and many children were becoming skilled in conversations en masse, and so it was a group discussion around a blanket, where the conversation finally turned to something Nick just couldn't resist.

Nick actually started the conversation, but he was speaking directly to the teacher next to him.

"I went to the mall with my grandpa, and …"

"Here, Nick, why don't you turn like this, toward all the kids, so everyone can hear your idea …" I suggested with a smile.

He began again. "Um, well, you see, I went to the mall with my grandpa and I …"

"I went to my grandpa's house, too," blurted out Jaren.

"I don't think Nick has finished yet …" interjected the respectful teacher, looking at Nick.

"Well … um … ya see … we kinda …" Nick was self-conscious for a moment, having to look at all the other kids.

Carli couldn't wait. "My grandpa lives in Florida and we're gonna go there and we're gonna bring the baby and we like to see Grandma and my brother will go too and we're gonna stay in a hotel and we're gonna swim in a pool and then …"

When she took a breath, the other teacher quickly and kindly interceded, "That's a lot of ideas you have. Thanks. I think I see that Jeremy wants to say something, too." The whole class knew that when Carli got going, it could be a l-o-o-ng wait for a break! And since everyone, almost, had a grandpa, this was indeed an interesting topic that Nick had begun. We wanted them all to have a chance.

"My grandpa is in Arizona," ventured Jeremy.

"Mine, too!" marveled Annie.

"Well, my grandpa lets me ride his lawn mower," stated Jennifer

"My grandpa lets me ride his golf cart ..." countered Sammy, "... all the way to the pool!" A pause while all pondered enviously. We waited. Then,

"I went with my grandad fishing," offered Jimmy.

"I went with my Opa fishing, too," added Milo.

"Me too," came several others.

"I went fishing ..." and it went on and on (these were, after all, Minnesota kids.)

"I caught a fish."

"I did, too."

"Me too."

"Me fish ..."

"A big one ... a crappy ... "

"I caught a big fish and a little fish ..."

Awed, and for once, speechless, Nick stared at his newly noticed associates. "Weh ... Weh ...Well, I never caught a fish IN MY LIFE!"

The teachers controlled their bemused chuckles. (His life, after all, has not been as long as a grandfather's; at four-years-old, he has a lot of fishing ahead of him.) Pulling ourselves together, we announced that, "while it's been fun hearing all your ideas, we know everyone would like to play in our room," pointing out the new pretend camping area, among other activities they could choose from.

But what we remembered, even more than the fishing tale, was the next comment of Nick's, as he turned to the admired Jimmy of the fishing grandpa ...

"Hey, Jimmy, let's play fishing ..." and he followed his new idol to the play fishing rods at the play boating area, where much imaginary trolling ensued over the next several days. Nick had discovered that shared ideas led to shared friendships with all kinds of people, not just grownups, and was on his way toward using his verbal skills for social growth.

THOUGHTS FOR TEACHERS

Conversation time: instead of 'circle time,' we call it a time together.

Sometimes, and in fact, often at the beginning of the year, this is snack time. What greater time to begin conversation skills? Or it could be sitting at a meeting place at the end of the day, after a hike together, or some outdoor play.

We start slowly in teaching children this kind of conversation. After all, some adults are not very good at it, either! One teacher asks the group a question about what they have done, and solicits ideas from them all, making sure that each child can see and hear the others and commenting occasionally when it becomes hard to hear. "I can't hear; we're all talking at once. Can you hold that thought, Josie, until Johnny has finished?" And so they learn, day by day, that it simply doesn't work when everyone talks at once, and that their ideas will be heard eventually. We coach them in openers, like "I have an idea" or "I want to say something" and we guide them to know when their comment is on the subject at hand or totally off in 'egocentric-land,' as often it is for this age group. If too many people talk at once, we announce, "We can't hear, can you?" and they soon learn that waiting until someone has finished, and then beginning, is the best way to be heard.

Conversation should be multidirectional.

Structure is important for conversation time. While sitting auditorium style fosters attention to the song leader, announcer, or book reader, it does not foster group interaction and listening to each other. Here, truly, a circle is the best. "Let's sit beside each other, so you're not in front of anyone," a teacher might say. "Make a circle" is difficult for a single child to understand from their egocentric point of view, so we might spread out a blanket for them to sit around.

As children gradually learn to increase their ability to speak to the whole group and to respond to each other, we begin seeing this directional change. Think of the teacher-directed group time, such as writing a group story or reading a book, as a triangle ... the teacher is at the point, and all ideas go toward her. Imagine directional arrows going up to the point. The direction shift, as children begin feeling comfortable with the conversation time, is arrows going across the circle, back and forth as though we were tossing a ball, with the teacher occasionally throwing it back, but hopefully not as much as the children. If you analyze your group times and discover that all the arrows are pointing to *you*, then it is not a group conversation.

The goal of conversation time is one of balancing the individual vs. the group.

As in much of school learning, conversation time also includes the need for spontaneity and optimal participation, which means that occasionally children will interrupt and not listen to others. We are helping children learn to balance their own needs to talk with the needs of the others. They learn this by listening, waiting until there's a time to speak, and eventually, sharing their ideas.

It's important to be sensitive to individual differences.

Consider, too, that not everyone talks easily in a group. The anguish experienced in childhood produced by waiting one's turn for the traditional 'show and tell' is remembered by many a formerly shy adult. We believe that a less formal conversational style at group time, when appropriate, creates comfort and interest in the more reticent children. A conversation comes to my mind when little Allie, who frequently froze rather than respond to a direct teacher question, and never blurted out anything in a large group, answered my question in the course of a group discussion about ... yes, grandparents, again. It was after spring break, and I knew she had flown with her family to visit grandparents in Florida. As the conversation rolled on about "going to Grandpa's," I asked her how she had traveled to visit her relatives. "We flied ... in a big plane ..." she couldn't resist telling about this exciting adventure. It wasn't a lot, but it was a step in the right direction!

Conversational skills are valuable life skills.

Some teachers may feel children are too young to learn conversational skills in school, but we believe that if they can listen to their teacher, they can learn to listen to each other. Furthermore, if they can wait for the teacher to call on them, they can also learn to wait until someone is finished so they can start. Child psychologists say that it is important to respect children and their ideas in order for learning to take place; educational researchers claim that children learn best by planning, choosing and being involved: if we believe this, then it is important to teach them to talk together.

THOUGHTS FOR PARENTS

Have meaningful conversations whenever possible.

When do we talk too much? Of course, we want to talk a lot with our children. When they are babies, we naturally babble on to them, and as they begin learning language we delight in each word they say, repeating back several more in return. Having meaningful conversations with our children is an important goal of many parents: we see it a way to teach, to build our relationships, to share our love.

However, children can become dependent on adult feedback.

As in any other relationship, language development is a matter of balance. We don't want to talk too much, so that our children become reticent listeners, or let them talk too much, so they become unable to listen to others. In the case of Nick, his grandparents and parents were right to encourage his natural inquisitiveness and talkativeness; it was simply time for him to learn he did not need the immediate reward of their approval and answers for his ideas and conversation to be valid. This is the benefit of a school for young children: early interaction with peers, as well as with other interested and interesting adults, so that the child becomes comfortable speaking, and listening, in a variety of settings.

Temperamental differences create variation in talkativeness in any family.

Keeping in mind the vast temperamental differences in people (some love talking, others are more content to be silent), it is important for *all* to be able to use language competently in order to share ideas and learn from others. We as parents can be good observers of our *own* children. We *can* respect their differences, sensitively, and allow them to learn within their temperamental parameters. Group conversations at home, as in talking around the family table, may be helpful in encouraging the quieter ones to talk and the talkative to listen, but above all they teach us to learn to listen to each other and to enjoy the exchange of ideas.

We can observe and encourage basic conversational rules in our children's language development.

When, in our encouragement of verbal ability in children, are we fostering rote repetition and attention-aimed comments? When are we allowing our children to interrupt our own needs as individuals to share ideas and points of our day? When are we interrupting them in return, or squelching their spontaneity? Observation is key as our children's ages and family constellation change, but the ancient rules of civilized conversation remain as a guide to human communication. At what age should we begin teaching the attitudes and skills of polite, interactive conversation? At the Children's Farm our experience has shown us it's never too early to start.

Adam: "We figured it out."

*An argument over toy boats
turns into a meaningful math lesson.*

"YOU'VE GOT MORE, SEE? 1,2,3,4,5. You guys have 5. You should give him one."

The voices reached across the room, rising from the water table, confident counting, and re-counting ... "4,3,5" followed by, "I don't have any, I need one," in a plaintive voice.

I supposed that Adam, a five-year-old tall and friendly fellow, had come to the aid of boatless Kent, who was barely four. "He doesn't have a boat. You guys have a lot. You should give him one," I heard him announce.

Mutterings ... then more counting followed. Adam, flanked by his agreeing buddy Martin, explained again, but the other two sailors, Zack and Michael, held their ground. "No, you give him one," they insisted.

Isn't it great the way Adam is helping Kent? I thought, as I meandered over to be sure the issue was settled without undue splashing of boats. Furthermore, isn't it great the way they're counting to settle the issue? observed my pedagogical side. This is real Learning Through Play!

And, indeed, it was, but when I arrived at the busy water table, I realized there was more here than just boat counting.

73

"See," Adam explained, in a patronizing voice to Zack and Mike, "you two have five boats there. Five is more than four. So you give Kent a boat." I wondered why this logic wasn't moving Zack and Mike and sidled closer to see if I could facilitate a moment of sharing.

Then I saw why Zack and Mike would not give in! Adam had three boats, and his friend Martin had four. Zack and Mike *knew* that together they had less than Martin and Adam together, but were at a loss to explain it to Adam. The words for addition weren't there yet!

"It looks like there's two ideas here. Let's figure this out." (My teacher words for resolving conflict.) Slowly and all together we began counting each person's boats. Then we counted together to add up Zack and Mike's boats (5) and Adam and Martin's boats (7). Soon all decided we could ask Martin, who had four, to give up one boat to the persistent Kent, still whining at the end of the water table. Reviewing this exchange, I used the words add, plus, and subtract (take away) to challenge and provide them with new words to think through future problems in their ever-expanding play.

Involved in the addition and subtraction, no one complained this time when Adam handed over the boat to Kent. Back to playing and splashing, but was it just my wishing, or was there a new grin on Adam's face? It wasn't about needing the boat, it was about solving the problem. Then, "We figured it out, guys," I heard him say as I turned away.

THOUGHTS FOR TEACHERS

Motivating activities can provide the foundations of math learning.

Counting can certainly be interesting when you add a motivating self-interest to the picture. The children persisted at this challenging 'word problem' because each wanted to play with the boats! Whether the actual math lesson sticks with them or not, the foundation is there. The understanding that problems can be negotiated with words, that numbers can be manipulated and put together to express reality, and, hopefully, the confidence that, "I can figure this out!"

Some math activities are planned, others come at 'teachable moments.'

So, do we teach mathematics in preschool? Absolutely, every day to involved and motivated youngsters. Sometimes it is a planned activity that we know will facilitate the learning of counting, such as making charts of numbers of birds seen, or adding up the money from the eggs we sold. Most of the time it is a matter of watching for that teachable moment, counting to compare, to share, to decide, to eat, to sing, to swing; and counting all children to be sure they know that they, too, need to be 'counted in' and that they and their ideas "count." We count chicks, eggs, crackers, books, ideas, and votes.

By the end of the year, we know that each child can count as high as the number of children in the class. Not only do they know about individual numbers, but about sets, and they see themselves as a part of a set which is the class.

It was late spring when a visitor had come over the hill to observe the school. The children were standing together by the granary, getting ready to be counted.

"See," called out four-year-old Peter to the visitor, "there are seventeen of us!"

THOUGHTS FOR PARENTS

Teach meaningful concepts in daily routines.

One time a parent of a prospective student, stopping by for a classroom visit, asked me, "Do you count?" I felt like asking her, "Do you?" Schools intentionally plan activities for children to learn counting, but this is only necessary because schools are to an extent (and some more than others) an artificial environment for children. In our daily life with children there are many times to teach numbers and a myriad of things to count in meaningful ways. I don't mean rote counting in order to memorize the order of the numbers, but the kind of *meanings* that make math count.

One-to-one correspondence (one foot, one shoe, two mittens, two hands) can be taught as a child learns to dress herself. Snack or meal times (two cookies, three cookies) are more occasions to learn numbers. Again, not the boring "there are 1-2-3-4-5 cookies," but the meaningful, "there are 1-2-3-4-5 cookies and there are 1-2-3-4 of us. Will we have enough?" Now that will get them thinking! The good old peanut butter sandwich at lunch is a great opportunity to teach half, whole, and quarters. Then cut the sandwich diagonally, for a lesson in conservation. (Most children will guess the triangle-shaped quarter is larger, until they catch on.)

Believe me, it works.

As a young parent on the farm I got into math games with my children as they gathered eggs and helped in the garden. We counted potatoes, peas, and tomatoes, and of course, eggs. Who knew that the three-year-old who dropped the bucket of eggs and then peered in to announce, "Three take away two really is one!" would one day become a nuclear engineer? I just knew she was learning her math. I do claim, however, that her insight about subtraction was the turning point in thinking about having a school on the farm.

It's exciting and fun teaching a child these insights.

Computer games and electronic learning notwithstanding, manipulating real items to count and to add and subtract is still the best way for children to learn numbers. This is the true meaning of learning through play. A child's parent *is* her first teacher — and what an exciting job it is. To see the 'light bulb,' the flash of understanding, to hear them say, "We figured it out," is what teaching is all about. Don't miss it!

Jeremy: "It's grown, it's grown!"

A child's eager manipulation of growing things starts him on a year's learning about the concept of growth.

JEREMY CAME RUNNING OUT to the teacher and children in the entryway, his voice high and chirping as he waved a tulip bulb, roots dangling in the air. "It's grown!' It's grown!' he cried. And indeed it had! There was a green tip on the pointy end and little white roots dangling down. We could see them as he swung it about!

It was the coldest part of winter. The children had hurried up to the schoolroom door, frosty breaths steaming as they stamped across the frozen slabs of the patio. It was way too cold to be feeding animals first thing in the morning, and possibly it would be a job for the teachers later in the day, unless that thermometer warmed up a few more degrees. Kicking off their boots and placing them on the boot shelf by the door, they had headed toward the coat hooks. No words were needed from the adults. By now children had learned that each person's clothes were their own responsibility. It only took a few times of missing their mittens and being the last one out for sledding to remember to put them carefully in their sleeves.

The children then busied themselves at peeling off their many layers. Small hands worked at eye hand coordination and finger dexterity. (What do children in California do for these gratifying lessons of skill? I've often wondered.) Those with one-piece snowsuits were able to zip themselves out more quickly, and soon were moving toward the waiting schoolroom, eager to begin play at their blocks, puzzles, or art projects. As Jeremy headed for the block corner he stopped to investigate the newly planted bulb garden, a large plastic tray with a couple inches of potting soil and about twenty bulbs of different categories. He remembered planting them, along with a teacher and four or five other children, the week before on another cold January morning. Then he made his miraculous discovery! They were up!!

Wow, neat, look! All gathered around to see, and Jeremy held it high, showing the white roots and green point. Soon the teacher suggested, tactfully, that since the bulb really needed to be in the soil to grow, he replant it. Together they tucked it back in, patted it down, and Jeremy squeezed the plastic bottle of water while his friends watched. They adjusted the stick with the sign, 'daffodil,' written on it, and then turned to start their block building. Jeremy and his friends were learning — learning about growing.

Through the winter and spring, they had further occasions to learn about growing. As each bulb sprouted forth and flowered, differences were noted, sizes compared, and colors of blooms were observed. One large pot on the table near the window held an amaryllis bulb. That miracle of winter growing lent itself especially to measuring, as a small card behind it, with a nearby marker, invited small hands to mark a line of latest growth. "Look, I made the mark, teacher. Now you write the number here, can't you see, it's grown?"

And who could forget seedlings, and the faithful listening and doing as teacher explained that these tiny seeds would sprout if we planted carefully and watered correctly? And so they tried, small fingers groping for tiny broccoli and tomato specks, gently patting with one finger in each hole of egg carton planters, squeezing water in each receptacle and placing the tray carefully on the window sill. A week went by, they'd almost forgotten, and then someone noticed, (or did they all?) the tiny green things starting up. They've grown! And grew and grew, 'til eager hands were finally able, permitted by sun's warming rays, to plant with guidance in the outdoor garden patch.

Then it was baby animal time on the farm. They started with eggs. Each child got to place one gently in the incubator, after bringing it up from the chicken coop where they had been carefully collected. Teachers turned on the mechanisms, explaining how important it was not to bump, and writing out the numbers, twenty-one in all, that would be needed for these eggs to hatch. Each day the children looked in the little window on the square plastic incubator, (and wondered, and waited, and counted.) Some forgot, but then the day arrived when cheeps and peeps were heard. The lucky ones watched the cracks get bigger, the persistent ones saw the chick burst out, so surprisingly wet and scraggly, but clearly alive and not an egg at all anymore. By the next school day, the soft and fuzzy chicks were running around, one-finger-pettable, as children learned the careful way to touch that seductive fluffiness. But how could it fit in the egg? It's bigger now, it's grown.

So, no wonder then, the children learned. It was early in the fall when the teachers had taped up that long piece of craft paper, and all had come over to have a mark placed on where tops of heads could reach. The teachers explained, "This is how tall you are today." Each child would point and show their name, and know, *that's me, that's where I am.*

That was a long time ago, so many days and seasons of learning had passed as understanding grew. This spring, when teachers pasted the long rolled-up chart back on the wall, Jeremy approached the line again. He turned and placing his finger above his head — much, much higher, he noticed. Pointing for the teacher to mark the spot, Jeremy crowed, "I've grown, I've grown!"

THOUGHTS FOR TEACHERS

Global concepts are formed early and provide foundations for further inquiry.

Global concepts like life cycles and growing things are the foundations of scientific understandings. That said, should we wonder why the majority of junior high school students find science uninteresting? If we never offer experiences with real and natural phenomenon, the world continues as one giant and mysterious technological bubble, about which there are no aspirations for understanding or glimmer of interest other than pushing the button or touching the screen.

Activities in our curriculum are designed to help children understand other concepts or processes of change as well. Our fall corn activities include not only harvesting, but also grinding corn meal and cooking corn muffins. Wood activities in the winter start with collecting fallen branches on a hike, then move in to sawing the wood into smaller pieces (well supervised but with *real* saws) and end with a nice warm bonfire to show the wonder of that "Wood Warms You Twice" story we read together.

And the 'ba-a-a to blanket' activities help show how something growing on a sheep can be changed by human effort, washed, carded, spun and woven, to turn it into warm wool blankets and hats. A spinning wheel offers a great way to wonder about the dynamics of speed and gears, twisting and changing things, when "we know where they came from."

I walked into the classroom one day to see the children begin the orange juice activity: sawing oranges in half to put in a giant and kid-friendly squeezer, the object being to show children where our orange juice comes from. A child looked up at me, confidently yielding a long cutting knife with his teacher's guidance, and proclaimed with a grin, "This is real!"

82

Teachers can plan to surround kids
with science in their classroom.

Schools can help make up for the deficit in our daily contact with the natural world, by bringing living things, both plants and animals, into the classrooms. Encouraged by teachers to manipulate, touch and wonder, young children need no prepared 'science lesson.' They will do the questioning and investigating as they play and work with the materials.

Teachers can comment on the play and show wonder and questioning themselves, but should avoid over explaining or giving too many pat answers. "Why is that little wheel going faster than the big one?" or, "I wonder if that mouse the cat caught is alive or dead?" Rather than a science 'unit,' plan for children to experience the science that is all around them in the ways children learn best, by doing! Cook it, build it, plant it, examine it, take it apart, count it and compare it — science is all around us!

THOUGHTS FOR PARENTS

Plants and animals offer many opportunities for understanding concepts.

"You'll grow, you'll get bigger." These concepts are sometimes hard to understand. A child feels small, everyone else is more capable, why try? Helping children appreciate their own growth and progress can give courage as they face new challenges each year. Having animals and growing plants in the home provide many benefits, including caring, responsibility, and aesthetics. Not the least of these is the grounding in science understandings which living things offer to young children living among them. Some indoor plantings, a small garden, or a fish in a bowl, can make our homes a place for wondering.

Let's keep the wonder alive.

Wonder is something children are born with. Just watch an infant inspect his new world. Can we 'un-teach it?' I think so. As Aldo Leopold wrote, "I wonder whether the process ordinarily referred to as growing up is not actually a process of growing down; whether experience, so much touted among adults as a thing children lack, is not actually a progressive dilution of the essentials by the trivialities of living." Things we grownups may take for granted, like plants sprouting, sunsets glowing, stars popping out are wondrous events for young children.

We parents can share and encourage this wonder in young children with excitement, not lecturing or putting down. We can try to keep alive that passionate learning, the kind that says, "wow, neat, look!" This is especially easy to do with everyday science concepts. Let's help remember the wonder of it all; it's an amazing world! And it's contagious, as we adults get to participate in their wonder and then experience that best miracle of all — the wonder of our own child's growth.

Part 3: Teaching to Individual Differences

Jack and David: "I'm bleeding ..." "I'm not!"

Teachers ponder the challenges of helping two children with opposite temperaments learn to be resilient and yet sensitive.

ISN'T IT INTERESTING how different children can be? Jack and David were both four-year-olds in their second year at the farm. As opposite in temperament as two children can be: Jack, thoughtful, competent, reserved, and undemonstrative; David, impulsive, outgoing, and emotional, but also competent, at least at physical chores. They clashed often in their first year at school, usually over issues of turf or toys.

How could I forget that day the year before when three-year-old Jack bit David? To Jack, it had seemed the logical thing to do, I'm sure. There was Jack, thoughtfully arranging his blocks as he planned out another massive parking garage, when David approached, wielding a large wooden truck and driving it enthusiastically, with great revvvvving, right up to the newly positioned blocks. It was also easy to understand the impassioned and wronged David, who had fled screaming from the scene of block destruction, wailing and crying bitterly, unable to be consoled, even though the bite was invisible to the observer. To the teachers it was disturbing to see Jack coldly sitting on the floor repositioning his blocks; it was equally disturbing to witness the intense emotion of David's response, which continued much longer than one would expect. For Jack, we wished some empathy and feeling, for David we wished some resilience so that he was not overwhelmed with his feelings. The usual teacher exercises in conflict resolution gradually helped teach Jack not to bite, and convinced David to stay away from Jack's blocks with his truck. Still they continued to squabble frequently. What was needed was not conflict resolution, but temperament adjustment, if that is possible.

On this fall day of their second year, the children were harvesting corn and squash out in the back garden. Crunchy, dried corn stalks bent, as twisting and turning, the children pulled the cobs off and chucked them into red wagons to pull to the corn crib. Others were busily rolling various colored squash to the wheelbarrows, where they would be brought to the play area to be counted and sorted. We were leaving the garden when I noticed Jack, standing still, looking silently at his hand, which was covered with blood.

Knowing children can be frightened by so much blood, I hastened to reassure and comfort him, but his face was clear, a wondering look in his eyes. A trip together to the bathroom to clean it off and put a bandage on the cut yielded no tears, or sign of dismay, nor could Jack really be sure how it had happened. He was crawling on something pokey, he thought, maybe. At the end of the day I explained the bandage to Jack's mom, who said, "Oh, he hardly ever cries over anything. It's kind of worrisome, I guess. Both of our kids seem to feel no pain!" She barely glanced at the cut as Jack climbed into her car.

Mmm, I mused. That certainly fit with Jack's other behaviors. He often appeared quite unconscious of the feelings of others. I remembered how, before he learned not to bite, he never seemed to show the slightest emotion or remorse when faced with his crying accuser. Did he not feel their pain because he was unaware of his own?

The same day that Jack cut his hand, David had wailed and cried for teachers' support on several occasions. Someone had pushed him, another had taken something from him, someone had called him stupid, once he tripped. Tears of anger or righteous indignation sprang to his face at the slightest provocation. We calmly reassured him, telling him he could handle it, giving him some words to say, and soon he was all smiles again.

Still, it had been a difficult day for him. Concerned that his intense emotion was interfering with other opportunities for learning, I called his mother that evening. Yes, David was such a sensitive child, his mother agreed, and she, too wished he wasn't so emotional about mishaps in his life. On the other hand, she commented on how sensitive he was to the feelings of others. He always fussed and worried about others, too. She spoke proudly of how caring and worried David had been about her recent childbirth. "Are you okay, Mommy?" he would ask. "Didn't the doctor hurt you?" he'd fretted.

I hung up thinking that worrying about Mom in this way was quite sensitive, but also scary for a four-year-old. Did David's sensitivity have an underlying fear? Could we help him feel more in control, more competent? He was still going to be sensitive, that was his temperament, but ... and that's when it hit me. In both Jack and David's cases, the issue was the same; not temperament adjustment, but optimal accommodation to their given natures.

THOUGHTS FOR TEACHERS

We wish for all children a healthy balance between temperamental extremes, but each child is unique.

Indeed, how do we teach children to be empathetic and sensitive, and yet also help them to be resilient and courageous in the face of occasional setbacks? If we teach them to be tough, how do they learn to feel the pain of others? If we teach them to be feeling, how do they learn to cope when the earth comes up and slaps them on the face when they fall down, literally and figuratively? Nevertheless, each child was experiencing some difficulty in coping with the challenges of school life, and the parents were both concerned. Devising some strategy for helping the children cope in a psychologically healthy way was important.

Teachers can work to help children be aware of feelings: theirs and others.

In Jack's case, we concentrated on teaching him to be aware of the feelings of others, and after the cut incident, of his own feelings as well. We occasionally asked him if he felt sad or angry, and how he thought others were feeling, both physically and emotionally. Stories were read to Jack and his class that encouraged discussion about and perception of feelings and emotions. Animal care was especially encouraged for Jack, with much cuddling of kitties, and animal feelings were discussed. Situations were devised at school in which Jack, with teacher encouragement and guidance, could help others younger or weaker than himself.

Teachers can also guide children in emotional self-control.

As for David, we worked hard at school to help him learn that he could cope, and that the intense emotion that so debilitated him at times could be turned to a rational purpose. We said things like "you could tell yourself that it will feel better soon," or "You could tell him some words about how you felt and explain to him what you want." We tried not to pay undue attention to minor wails, to communicate that we had the confidence that he could and would be able to recover on his own. Competent, strong jobs that David could accomplish well were planned for him to encourage his perception of efficacy.

THOUGHTS FOR PARENTS

Each family is a unique blend of temperaments and values.

What part of these differences is temperamental and unchanging, and how much taught? Is the child's reaction "created" by the parental response, or is the parental response tailored to the child's basic temperament? Parental values could be significant in considering these two children, as well. David's mother was a sensitive individual herself and valued raising a sensitive, caring child. Jack's mother seemed to value rationality and coping skills. Whether these attitudes were based on a shared genetic temperament or an intentional environmental climate (nature vs. nurture) is hard to determine.

Knowing which came first may not be important by the time they enter school. Each family makes choices based upon what they think is important for their own children. This is why it is so important for teachers, caregivers, and parents to communicate; not to change values or fight temperaments, but to help each other understand and to come up with appropriate plans for helping children cope with others who are different from themselves

Parents can help unemotional children to recognize and value emotions.

We discussed our strategies at school with Jack's mother and she decided to give Jack some chores around the house where he could be helpful and caring to his little sister (with supervision). She also decided to share her own feelings more openly when Jack was with her and name feelings to Jack as they might come up in the family. She still loved how rational Jack was and we talked about ways to share some explanations of emotions with Jack that he would understand. ("Some people really feel sad, mad, etc. ... when ...")

Parents of sensitive children can guide them toward better self-control.

We communicated our plans to David's parents who were dealing with his intense emotion on an exhausting twenty-four-hour level. They were working on their own methods of discussing and explaining his frustrations to David as they occurred. They realized that they might be 'over talking' and began to recognize the value of exuding confidence by sometimes allowing him to cope on his own. They still loved how sensitive David was but tried to help him turn his sensitivity toward caring about others and to channel his emotions into positive outlets like talking or drawing pictures.

Hopefully, children with differing temperaments can learn to get along.

There is a 'happy ending' to this story of Jack and David. While they continued irritating each other throughout the times they were at the Children's Farm, these two boys went on to attend the same elementary school, where they found themselves to have more in common than they realized in other important ways. By the time they were in second grade they were best of friends. As David's dad came to pick up David's younger brother at our school, he told us that the boys still reminisce about their great times together at the Children's Farm! And sometimes David says, "Jack, remember when you bit me?" and they laugh and laugh.

Mara: "Hey guys, try this!"

*Individual differences are more important
than gender assumptions.*

MARA WAS TALL, almost five, talkative and active. Her dark eyes shone with enthusiasm as she joined the new class in September. She quickly made friends with the other girls, directing the pretend play corner, and joining in singing and story times with ease.

So upon hearing a wail coming from the schoolroom after a few weeks, I was surprised to find it was Mara. As the director, I consulted with the teachers, Sam and Jenny. "You know, from my first impression, she didn't seem the one who would dissolve into tears or be fearful," I remarked.

"Well, either she didn't get her way or her picture didn't turn out the way she'd planned it. Or she dropped her wood creation on the way to the parking lot. She seems to need us to fix anything that goes wrong," commented her teachers.

As we observed Mara over the next few weeks, we wondered what the issue was, for she usually appeared to have enough confidence both indoors and out. The teachers noted that she was remarkably strong and coordinated and was one of the better swingers, jumpers, and climbers; not that we gave out grades for physical prowess, but it was obvious that she was stellar in the class. When heading down to the barnyard, meeting at the big rock to go for a hike, or running up the hill past the farmhouse on the way to the waiting place at the steps, Mara was almost always leading the pack.

One day I took a teacher's place for the morning, and we had come in from a hike. It was a muddy path, she was racing a few other kids, boys mostly, and slipped, getting mud on her dress.

Oh, did I mention she often wore a dress? Very few children did at our school, especially since we had issued that five page 'Clothes to Wear to the Children's Farm' booklet on the first day of class. In it we stated our belief that children needed to wear comfortable play clothes, so that they were unhampered by fussing and worrying about their clothes.

We also remarked that parents of girls, especially, might pay particular attention to choosing shoes and play outfits, since the choices were fewer. Girls' boots are often less sturdy, their jackets are often less warm and their jeans less durable. In our culture, notwithstanding women's liberation beliefs, there is still a strong emphasis on females looking attractive in their clothes, or at least pink and frilly. Our booklet cautioned parents to choose carefully among simple clothes for children to wear to farm school.

On that muddy day, Mara's mother, a well-dressed, thin, and attractive woman, frowned at the site of that dirty streak on the dress. She rolled her eyes and dabbed at the mud as Mara climbed quickly into their new minivan. I had my usual internal reaction to some people's view of 'dirt.' *It's not dirt; it's soil, good, healthy soil!* And then on to thoughts like, *What does she think we are doing here at school? This isn't about being pretty here, it's about learning!* My thoughts went unvoiced, of course.

Mara's mother looked like she was going to say something, but then she stopped, perhaps remembering our conversation at fall parent teacher conferences the week before. Barbara, the mother, had raved about how much her daughter loved coming to school, how much she was learning, and especially, she had noticed she was doing less of that crying and whining that so irritated her family. The teacher had countered that, yes, we thought we were hearing less of that, too. We shared with the mother our approach to generally ignore the wails if we thought she could cope, and avoid rushing over; didn't she agree? (hint, hint)

"Uh, yes, I see, "Barbara had nodded. "Maybe we've been doing too much fussing over her when she cries at home." And then added, "You see, she's our only girl ..." (What's that got to do with it? thought the teacher, but Barbara's comment now added a clue to the mystery of Mara's inability to cope.)

As fall turned into winter, Mara increasingly enjoyed the outdoor physical activities. Hanging upside down on the swings became easier as children were wearing snow pants or wind pants. I particularly remember the day after the round bales were delivered by a neighboring farmer, two long rows of five-foot-high bales stretched out in the pasture. The teachers had debated how, or whether, to use these for outdoor play. I joined in on the conversation, suggesting that the maze-like intrigue of going in and out the bales would prompt many active games of hide and seek that all would enjoy. "And besides, they're really too high for anyone to climb on," I claimed.

"I bet Mara will get right up on them," teacher Jenny contributed.

"Well, with the snow on the ground now, it looks safe enough. If someone is coordinated enough to climb up, they probably won't fall off. Let's just see what they do, but don't help anyone climb up there who can't do it on their own." Agreeing, teachers Sam and Jenny went out to start the day.

Sure enough, it was only twenty minutes later when I arrived at the gate to see a picture I will keep in my mind. While other children played hide and seek or tentatively climbed the mesh wrapped hay bales, Mara was high above them, leaping from bale to bale, ballerina style, arms extended, toes pointed — confident and safe,

As she gained in confidence outdoors, it seemed the real Mara was coming to the surface indoors, as well. She only occasionally fell into her old habit of pouting or bursting into tears when things didn't go her way. Was it the example of the others she was playing with? Was she just "growing out of it?" Or was it that the role of the helpless girl was less useful or necessary now that she had discovered her strengths? I believe that it was.

The next month I was again assisting in Mara's class. We were playing in the hayloft, for the winds of January were blowing strongly and the children needed some energy releasing exercise (a large padded cell is another definition of our hayloft.) Children were jumping on stacked rectangular bales and sliding on the boards, but Mara was over next to the high stack of straw, off limits for climbing since they were too slippery (and expensive).

She had discovered a new way to play. She got the idea to do a handstand up against the tall pile of bales, kicking up her feet, and remaining there, backed against the straw wall, facing toward the frolicking kids. Then, "Hey guys, try this!" Soon the whole class was participating, flopping hands down, kicking feet up, and trying to emulate this unique way of looking at the world!

Henry, wrapped in blue snowsuit and big red scarf, stood aside in awe. New to the school that month, he was just three and a half; and for then, at least, he could only watch with envy. I observed as he gradually edged closer to the upside-down Mara, where he quietly asked, "Are you a boy or a girl?"

The happy hand stander didn't hear him. Or if she failed to answer, perhaps it was because, really, it made no difference.

THOUGHTS FOR TEACHERS

Between gender groups of children, individual differences are more important than group stereotypes.

I would be lying if I denied that more boys than girls are first to run up the hill to the schoolroom. And I would be also lying if I claimed that there is a significant behavioral difference between boys and girls. Let me explain. Over the years, if I had I charted the boys versus the girls on hill racing, the mean, average distance would surely show boys as not only speedier but also more interested in getting there first. In the same way, I could show that more often than not, a girl was bringing up the rear, not caring how fast she went or not wanting to get her pink shoes scuffed. That said, I would also claim that each year there is an individual girl who is always first, and an individual boy who is always last.

It is important for teachers to remember that on *any* issue of group statistical difference between classes of children, individual variations are always greater than mean class difference. The solution? Never treat any children as a class, and always remember that each child is an individual.

In our society there are often pervasive gender outlooks to be aware of, like parent mindsets of 'boys will be boys,' to simple, everyday naming such as, "boys and girls ..." when teachers want to gather a group together. At the Children's Farm, we are careful not to exacerbate characteristics or limit possibilities in how we treat children and what our expectations are for them. We call our groups 'friends, people, everyone, helpers,' but not "boys at the table, come on over!" The naming of genders when they are totally irrelevant to the message only impresses observing young children that their gender must be important.

Gender differences should not influence our expectations for young children.

Genetic temperaments, physical age and stamina, and cultural background all contribute strongly toward the individual differences that children bring to school. At the Children's Farm teachers encourage boys to help cook, play dress up, and cuddle with the kitties with the same sense of purpose that we have when we encourage girls to build with blocks, solve science problems, and climb and run fast outdoors. Physical exercise, opportunities to feel strong, to compete, and to rise to new challenges are needs of all children, not just one gender. So are the needs to care, to cry, and also to ask for help when needed. When we are dealing with young children, gender issues just don't count and shouldn't enter into our interactions.

THOUGHTS FOR PARENTS

The messages we give children
in daily interactions can be powerful.

I remember a conversation I had with a parent about her daughter's "popularity" in school. The child was, well, chubby. As far as I could see, none of the children had even noticed or cared to comment, but the mother was concerned that we be vigilant in making sure no one teased her daughter about her size. Perhaps remembering episodes in her childhood, I'm thinking probably in elementary school, she lectured me on making sure we taught all the children that it was what was inside that counted. No problem there, I thought, we are really all too busy learning and playing and working at our school to worry about individual differences of a physical nature.

The next day the chubby little girl arrived at school. "I'm pretty today," she said. "I have a new dress on." So much for the 'beauty is only skin deep' theory! The fact was, her mother didn't really believe it, either, and had 'armed' her daughter with the prettiest clothes she could find, in order to make sure she would feel confident. Well-intentioned, but still giving the message that appearances count. (At least for girls!)

Since that conversation, I have been careful in my teaching to never comment on the clothes a child is wearing. My response to the little girl in the 'pretty' dress, "Why, you look so friendly with that big smile you're wearing." And if the girls feel pressure to be 'pretty,' what messages do parents give when they send little boys to school with 'tough guy' action figure shirts. Are we "arming" them for a preconceived role as well?

This was confirmed to me years ago by the mother of a boy who was very enamored of Ninja Turtles, and who always wore his 'fighting turtle' shirt to school. "Yes, I encourage his interest in the Turtles. He's such a shy child, I think it will give him a way to fit in with the other little boys."

**Parents can help children develop
positive feelings about their gender
and their possibilities as individuals.**

Anxiously trying to figure out what is important in the big world around them, children look to peers, to TV, to older siblings, but especially to parents for those messages of what it is to be a girl or a boy. Let's consider the gender related values and goals we really believe in, and teach by example and by words.

"Are you a girl or a boy" is indeed a valid question for a three- or four-year-old. It is worthy of thoughtful answers, answers that don't limit a girl's perception of herself as a strong, coping person or a boy's self-image as a caring and sensitive person. It is important that we consider individual differences and encourage every child to make the most of all his or her talents, gender notwithstanding.

Janelle: "..."

Teachers plan to meet the needs of a child who never talks.

HER PURPLE-JACKETED ARMS held straight at her side, the curly-haired four-and-a-half-year-old stood stiffly in the center of the barnyard. *Oh, oh*, I thought, there she was, just watching ... silently.

"What will you do, Janelle?" I asked. "Some people are feeding the rabbits, others are looking for eggs. Or you could hold cats over by the barn?" I motioned to a group of three sitting on the hay pile, passing a patient cat back and forth.

A look, then she looked away, as if to say, *Don't ask me anything*. I helped some others with water for the rabbits, but I was thinking, what to do about Janelle? To join in activities on the farm, to be with the children; these were things we wanted for Janelle. We invited her along with the others, but Janelle ... well ... she was shy. No, it was more than shy. Janelle refused to talk. We'd seen her working hard at her effort to remain silent here at school. She'd been here since September, and according to her parents at conference time in November, she liked school. We'd heard her talk to her father, handsome and smiling in his big shiny truck, when he picked her up after school. How much energy she must have been using to avoid talking here! And why?

When she first started, she joined in with the others, held hands often with little Danielle and helped with chores and activities. We thought, any day now, she'd just talk. She'd forget herself and it would just come out and then she'd be talking.

Six months had passed, and it seemed she avoided doing anything. Was it because she was afraid she'd talk? Did she avoid activities as her defense against talking? And why didn't she want to talk here at school?

I made up my mind. I wouldn't let her stand there any longer. As I do most every day, I finally went over and directly asked her, "This is a really heavy bucket. Can you help me take it to the cow?" A nod. A look (was it relief?) and we were off together to the cow. Side by side, we tipped it in. I tried not to talk too much. *Let's just be together*, I thought. I wouldn't let her be alone. I wouldn't let her avoid us any longer.

We strolled down to the play area. "Let's see what's happening," I said. Some children were carrying wood beams from the sandbox to the blacktop, arranging them in house shapes and balancing on them. We watched them together. I walked on one, then invited her to try it. She followed behind me. I stumbled, I laughed, she looked … Was that a trace of a smile? I thought so.

"Let's get another one!" I invited Danielle and Jared to help us. All four got a beam from under the granary. We all carried it over. The children put it down and I stepped back … would she join in? Yes, a bit. She touched the beam with her foot, watching the others intently. This had been my strategy with Janelle: start a task with her, try to involve one or two others, then back off and let it happen with the kids. If she talked, I thought it would be with the kids, when she was sure the teachers weren't watching. What was her investment in not being "caught" saying anything?

It was the same story after we went indoors. I saw Janelle watching us plant seedlings. Everyone would get to take home a cup of planted seeds. Other children came over and asked to plant; at that time, I didn't even care if Janelle talked, but I would like to see her take the initiative to come over to do something she clearly wanted to do. Yet she hung back.

I asked the room in general, "Does anyone else want to plant now? There's space at the table ..." She looked and looked and stayed at the doorway. Finally, again, I got up for something else (a ploy) and then pretended I had just noticed her in passing. "Oh, Janelle, I bet you'd like to plant. Come right on over." I acted as if I assumed she'd love to plant, and indeed, she came right on over! What was different? Why did she need to be individually invited? While I told her what to do, she silently and capably wrote her name on the cup, poked a hole in the bottom, filled the cup, and planted the seeds. As Janelle watered hers with a waiting squeeze bottle, Ned started his seedling. He watched her take her flowerpot over to the window sill and turned to me.

"She's not deaf, is she?" he commented.

"Huh?" said I, surprised.

"She's not ... Janelle ... she hears what you say."

"Right," I agreed, smiling. Ned noticed that Janelle must have understood my directions, or she couldn't have accomplished the job so capably. What else had he noticed?

"She just doesn't talk," he continued. At the nearby art table, two children were cutting and pasting.

Janelle joined in time to hear, "Yeah, she has a voice."

"She just doesn't talk here," said another.

"She's shy," added a third.

"Sometimes I'm shy, too," continued the first. Janelle, the subject of their commentary, continued silently cutting her piece of paper, looking up and down.

"Is this where I put my name?" asked Ned, changing the subject as a four-year-old does best; completely.

THOUGHTS FOR TEACHERS

We use an 'Issues and Ideas' plan to think through behavior problems.

Every year there are some children who are particularly mystifying. At our school if we find that when we are frequently thinking about a particular child, discussing events of the day, or repeatedly planning with that child in mind, then we know it's time to write up an 'Issues and Ideas' sheet, and also, to consult with the parents. This form we have prepared for teacher use helps us clarify between teachers what the problem or puzzling behavior is: the 'issues.' Then we list possible causes and related teaching approaches: the 'ideas.'

The 'issues' section briefly defines the problem and lists possible causes.

In Janelle's case the issue was complicated by the fact that not talking was one problem, one which we were willing to be patient and optimistic about, given our knowledge that she spoke capably at home and also, because of our earlier observations, confirmed by parents, of her interest in other children and the school activities. The real issue more recently was her avoidance of doing things, the hanging back and literally 'cutting off her nose to spite her face,' in this way depriving herself of both the learning of the activities and the company of the other children who we were hoping would help her talk. *Did she read our minds? Does she find herself weakening, and so resists? Have her parents been encouraging her to talk at school?* This may be good, but it may be backfiring in her choosing to stay in the 'shy' role because of the attention it affords her. Also, we noticed lately that her grandmother has been bringing her to school; *does Grandma foster that shyness in her eagerness to make Janelle happy?* These are some of the possible causes we wrote down.

106

The 'ideas' section proposes possible plans.

The bottom half of the sheet has room for ideas: what to try that we haven't already tried? We came up with two ideas:

1) *Pair her with another child, but not a talkative one.* We'd tried talkative children like Ned, Danielle, and Kelsey. They all liked her (why?) but lately had taken to mothering her and talking for her (everyone likes a listener?) Perhaps if she had a younger child to talk with, one she'd have to help and show things to, as she must do at home with her younger cousin. We decide that Kole, our youngest, would be a likely choice, and plan to pair them for an occasional job or activity together next week.

2) One of our two new baby sheep is much more 'shy' than the other. We thought we'd *have a class project to try to "teach" this sheep to be less hesitant,* to like us. Maybe we'd take some pictures of kids hand-feeding it, and write a little book about the sheep who is 'shy.' We hesitate to label what Janelle is doing as 'shy'; labels have a way of being self-fulfilling prophecies. Is there another word we could use to describe the sheep?

Parents are always consulted when we are creating an 'issues and ideas' plan.

The last part of the 'Issues and Ideas' plan includes a phone call, or conference if appropriate, with the parents. We need parents' input and suggestions about the behavior of their child at school. It is not our intent to pry into things happening in Janelle's life which may contribute to her school behavior. After all, we are teachers, not child psychologists. Instead we use the 'rule of thumb' test: Would we be remiss if we did not share with her parents our concerns and our particular plans for Janelle?

THOUGHTS FOR PARENTS

Teachers welcomes parents' input regarding special concerns.

When discussing how a child is doing with teachers, parents can be a big help in sharing their understanding of their child. If a child's teachers are working on a certain issue at school, parents may be able to advise them if it is a particularly stressful time for the child at home or if parents think teachers should try a different approach based on their understanding of their child.

The child's behavior is her own responsibility; we can't fix it.

When teachers share their concerns about issues and ideas for helping a child, this is not a request that parents discipline or reward the child at home for behaviors at school. The teachers at the Children's Farm are not asking parents to 'fix' the child's behavior at school, any more than parents would expect the teachers to get their child to go to bed on time or eat his peas at home. The child's behavior at school is the child's responsibility.

Parents and teachers can work together to help change the child's perception and goals.

It's important to remember that only the child can change the child's behavior. Caring and responsible adults can work to change the child's perceptions, try to change the child's goals, give the child insights of alternative possibilities. In this sense, it is valuable for both parents and teachers to communicate, not necessarily to do the same thing, but so that each will understand the child better. For instance, it really helped us to know that Janelle spoke fluently at home, and also that she did not speak in other settings either, such as Sunday School.

Our communication with the parents went smoothly. We

hoped they were not trying too hard to get her to talk in new places, either by cajoling or by threatening, which might have caused her to be so self-conscious about speaking. We tried our two ideas with the parents' agreement and made daily efforts not to enable Janelle in her helplessness, all while respecting her choices and showing her we cared and were interested in her. This is the best we could do for Janelle, and her behavior was her choice. Janelle finished out the entire school year, never having spoken to either a child or a teacher at our school.

Kurt: "You're dumb ... you idiot!"

A child's increasingly angry behavior becomes a challenge.

"YOU'RE DUMB ... YOU IDIOT ..." He repeated the words coldly, slowly, as if waiting to see what reaction there would be. I silently carried the kicking boy, a sturdy five-year-old with crew cut and usually smiling face, not smiling now. I needed to carry him close to my body, with my arms around him and his face away from me, knowing that he sometimes bit. I tried not to huff and puff too much, as we rounded the farmhouse hill and started down the wide, wooden steps leading to the schoolroom. There would be time enough for words once we reached the entryway. I felt his fingernails on my arms, trying to scratch, yet he struggled only a little as though he really didn't want to get away, just wanted to hurt me, hurt someone, hurt anything. Kurt was angry!

Somehow I opened the schoolroom door and put Kurt down. He stomped in ahead of me, arms crossed and face strained in fury. He stood rigidly, looking around the room, the clothes hooks, the water table, empty now because it was springtime and the playing was done outdoors on nice days. The room was quiet and cool. I controlled my huffing and took some deep breaths.

What would I say? What could I say that hadn't been said already? *Kurt, we like you, Kurt, you're a great kid, Kurt, it isn't okay to kick and hit and push other people. Kurt, I'm here to help you. Kurt, what's your problem?*

Kurt glared at me. I looked back, trying not to appear angry, because I really wasn't ... just sad. "You look really mad," I finally ventured.

"You're dumb, they're all dumb," Kurt insisted, clenching his fists, and swinging his foot a bit.

"Why?" I asked.

"They just are. I'm gonna really hurt them next time."

"Well, I won't let you do that," I countered calmly. "I need to make sure it's safe for everyone here."

"I hate safe!" exclaimed the angry Kurt. He began roaming the entryway, swinging his arms from side to side. I sat down on the floor, as if to converse.

"This is a problem," I said. "What should we do?"

Kurt started ripping at the poster on the door. I reached him and held him in my arms.

"Let go of me."

"I need to hold you so you won't tear our stuff," I said. I sat on the floor, arms around him from behind in an enclosing, but safe, hug. Once again, "It's not okay to push any kids." Silence.

I went on, "When Sophie came to the sandbox she wanted to play with you. She likes you."

"Well, I don't like her. I didn't want her there."

Slowly, quietly, I began talking. "We like you here, Kurt. You look really angry, but it's not okay to hurt others. If there's a problem, say some words to the kids, or call me to help. Now, I brought you inside, because it's not safe there outside until you calm down. What will you do inside to help yourself to not be mad? You could try a picture or play with the clay." I gestured into the empty classroom, releasing him slightly as I felt him relaxing.

We heard the thuds of approaching feet as the rest of the

class arrived at the door for some indoor play. Kurt quickly walked over to the clay table and got busy, as if to cover up when the other children, entering now, would see him inside. As he pounded and pressed and pushed on the clay, I could see his anger, voiced to me but not reciprocated, begin to dissipate. When some others sat down beside him, he barely glanced at them, but soon began talking and smiling as they vied with each other to create the 'ugliest monster.' I began to breath normally again. Another crisis with Kurt was past, at least for a while.

I continued to think about Kurt as I went about my normal role of helping, listening, and commenting to all the others. I watched him throughout the morning. After leaving the clay table, he went to the picture table, where he sat and worked carefully on two detailed pictures, coloring in the people carefully and writing his full name on both. This is where we've seen Kurt be so happy and successful, I thought. He really is focused on paper and pencil tasks. I remembered how we had worked with him to write words for his word envelope, how eagerly he wrote EGGS on our egg sale sign, how interested he was in stories. I wish I had more time to teach him to read, I thought. I know he's almost there, but in our two morning-a-week sessions, outside more now that it's springtime, there isn't the time. Reading would be a way for him to feel big, as big as his three older brothers, the "tough, bad" ones he brags about to the other kids.

I knew the older brothers, who had all attended our school a few years ahead of Kurt. Active kids they were, a bit more physical than many, but we were always able to teach them the way to be with other kids. They were never angry like Kurt. Their mom seemed unperturbed; "that's the way boys are," she declared, and indeed, hers were. After a few explanations of how hitting was not okay here, they seemed to learn what was expected of them at school and had passed through the years without too much ado.

And Kurt had started out that way, too. He was an interested and participating class member since he began last September. Our only foretelling comment to his parents at the fall parent conference was about his quickness to anger; he sometimes got mad for what seemed to be small things, and would make an angry face or stomp away, but he always recovered quickly. I remember the time a teacher was explaining to the class what 'the plan' for the day was and at the end Kurt said, "Well, I don't like your plan!" but he still did do it. Kurt loved to help on cooking and snack preparation and was always an involved participant in singing, stories, and other group activities.

However, in February and early March he began to arrive at school "grouchy" and to want to take this out on others. For a while it was the 'word of the day' — punk, idiot, pervert, or worse — which he would try on others for their reaction. He would yell at other kids and say he didn't like them, even those he had been playing happily with days and even minutes earlier. He would also resent and argue with teachers' directives, as if to provoke a face off. "I won't come in, I'm not done ..." as in, "make me." And "boring, boring, boring," he would say when we began a story, even though he usually stopped because we ignored him and, in spite of himself, he loved stories. As we entered March his anger had turned physical and we frequently had to intervene to protect other children. About this time, we began to document his behavior and we contacted his parents about our concerns.

His parents had seen his angry moods at home, much earlier than we had. They had "tried everything" as they said, from cajoling, talking, explaining, yelling and, yes, even spanking. I had mentioned how we were explaining to Kurt how hitting was not okay, and that we were removing him from where he could hurt others if the situation demanded it. I also shared our proactive goals for Kurt: to help him feel bigger and more in control by giving him choices wherever we could, by giving him lots of opportunity to be helpful and useful, such as food preparation and chores, and by working with him on areas where he excelled, such as reading, writing, drawing. Were there any things they could do at home to support these goals as well, maybe some special project? His mother agreed he loved to help her cook, but his brothers teased him about it. I suggested perhaps his mother could work with him on letters, writing, something special and exciting he could be proud about. She didn't know, she already spent so much time with him, he was so demanding and was driving her nuts. What could I say? Two and a half hours at school was taking a lot out of us teachers as well. We agreed to talk again in a week or so.

By the end of March things had not gotten much better. We were spending more time outdoors, which often is easier for a physical child, because the restless pent-up energy of winter can be released. But pent up anger, that was much harder to supervise outdoors. We found that the sandbox became a place of aggression for Kurt, needing a teacher present at all times. On a hike, we had to be sure to be directly behind him, to watch for pinches and punches whenever he thought someone might 'budge' or take his space. And at the end of the day, walking up the hill or out to the cars, he would sometimes just stomp, hard, on the foot of a child, usually one younger than him, and then laugh at the surprised cry of pain he caused. Another conference with the parents was held, in which time we expressed our concern about safety issues and suggested they consider some outside help for Kurt. We offered a list of community resources such as counselors and child psychologists. "Oh, no, we're not ready for that yet, we think he'll come around," had been the response.

Now I watched as Kurt helped prepare the snack for the day. Carefully spreading butter on the bread with the teacher, he proudly told her, "You know, I cook with my mom at home." He couldn't know that while we were glad to help him feel big by helping us, we were also keeping him out of the hubbub as the other children cleaned up the room, something that was just too difficult to monitor with an angry child on the loose. And when he and the teacher he was working with finished preparing snacks, we had already begun singing, so that he didn't have a chance to shout, "This is dumb," as he sat down with a teacher next to him. You see, I thought, we could make it work for Kurt, it just took constant surveillance and one-to-one attention. How could we handle that and still meet the needs of the other sixteen children in the class?

I thought about how this day had begun. It was the first day back after spring break and Kurt had arrived in a happy mood, showing off his new Hot Wheels car to the kids in the parking lot before he gave it to his mom to keep while he was at school. He talked merrily to the teacher about his new toy, how great it was. My heart sank. Kurt's mother had called me the night before. They had begun a new program at home, recommended by a friend, (so much for my child psychologist suggestion!) She and Kurt had gone shopping, and he had picked out six or seven new toys that he really wanted. Then they had put them in a box at home. They'd made a list of things he was not to do … no hitting, no calling names, etc. … and she was sure Kurt understood the goals. At the end of each day, if he had been good, he would choose a toy from the box. I felt like repeating Kurt's remark, "I don't like your plan," but of course, it was her choice what to do at home about his behavior at home. I did tell her we would not want to give a 'good/bad' report to her each day about Kurt at school, because we were not comfortable with how that might affect the rapport we had here with Kurt.

As for that morning, 'the plan' was to have children work in pairs to take feed to the chickens. Kurt raced ahead of his younger partner Nathan, dumped the feed eagerly, and gathered as many eggs as he could. But then, he accidentally dropped a couple. He roughly turned to Nathan, saying it was his fault, and I appeared quickly to bolster the trembling Nathan, both of us expecting some violence. Seeing me, Kurt said nothing more, but looked at me as though to say, *Uh, oh, there goes my prize.* He stomped toward the sandbox, no one was there, and I thought, *well, we'll let him be alone to cool off over there.* Maybe he was really trying, if only to gain that next toy. A few minutes later, some other children joined in, and they all began playing together. At least until the hapless Sophie had arrived; he'd decided he didn't want her, and had pushed her down.

How could the distant goal of a prize, already maybe jeopardized anyway, possibly keep him from that anger he needed to show? I knew that the behavior modification program his mother had planned was too small, too late, for too large a problem. Yet, we couldn't keep this up at school for another two months. How could we keep the other children safe? Already we were hearing from concerned parents whose children were complaining about Kurt's behavior toward them. I had a responsibility to these other children ... I thought ... I thought ... *we might have to ask Kurt to withdraw from the school.*

Kurt was singing now, with eyes alight, freckled face turned toward me and the guitar as all together we sang about five green and speckled frogs, glub, glub ... he loved the glub, glub part ... How could I give up on the great successes Kurt had had here, the times he said "thank you" to kids, the good ideas he shared, the ways he could be helpful? I couldn't let him leave in failure.

Then it was time get our outdoor jackets. I was putting away the guitar, the other teacher, Sam, was helping some children with zippers, and "You butthole" ... "Wa-a-a." I turned to see Kurt flicking his jacket at Nathan cowering in the corner. With no comment, I led Kurt by the hand into the schoolroom, knelt down beside him and said firmly, "Stay right here so it's safe." I left to help straighten a sleeve or two back in the entryway. Ignored, Kurt crouched down on

117

the floor, arms crossed, and stared at the floor. I imagined he planned to stay there, so that we would have to carry him out to the waiting cars.

The other children gathered cozily on the entryway floor around a large chart with three pictures on it. It was time to count the votes for the name of our new calf. Each child had earlier marked a line under the name he had wanted. As, all together, the group began counting, Kurt tried and tried to keep his head down in disdain, but he … he really wanted to see the pictures, to count the votes himself. His head came up, his face relaxed. (We pretended not to notice.) He couldn't help himself, and inched toward the door where he peered in. As Sam's finger pointed to each 'vote' and the children counted, his head bobbed in agreement, and finally he shouted out a number with the rest. Much as he had tried to banish himself from the group, and indeed we had banished him, counting was just too interesting to him. After the voting was counted and the calf was pronounced to be, yes, another Blackie, the children went to the shelf just inside the classroom to get their pictures, the very spot where Kurt was perched. Seeing them coming, he glanced at the pictures, and reading Nathan's name, "Here, this is yours," I heard Kurt's friendly voice as he handed Nathan his picture. Kurt then picked up his own two pictures, and along with his classmates, calmly walked down the path to the waiting cars.

His grandpa picked up today. "Hi, Kurt," he said with a big grin. "Were you good today?" Kurt silently got into the car and they drove away. *Was he good? Which time?* He was good a lot of times, but not all the time. How does a kid answer something like that?

That does it, I thought. We only had the rest of spring. I couldn't end it with the family like this. I'd get an extra person, maybe our student teacher or a former teacher part time, somehow cover it for two more months. Kurt needed us, what we could give him. This might be the only place!

THOUGHT FOR TEACHERS

Understanding emotions,
we know it is important not to return anger.

There's no place for anger for a teacher. An angry child often tries to get others to reciprocate; this justifies to him that his anger is okay and gives an excuse to show the fury he feels. While we want to reflect normal reactions of human beings (as in 'I am upset'), still, when we become aware of WHY the child is calling us names, we understand how important it is to remain firm but not angry.

Build on the positives.

Every child has positive aspects to capitalize on. We can't solve the anger, it wasn't caused at our school, but we can make our school a place where new successes can be had, where new relationships can be established, where new possibilities are offered. Coaching in problem solving skills and setting of clear behavior limits are made easier when we can offer interesting and challenging ways to behave as an alternative. Physical challenges, helping jobs, and interesting learning opportunities keep children busy with successes so that, hopefully, there is less and less time for failures.

Daily documenting of problem behavior
helps all to understand the issues.

Work with the family whenever you can. This was a family we knew, with whom we had good rapport. Even if we disagreed on methods, we could communicate. Nevertheless, as things got difficult with Kurt, we started documenting his behavior in writing each day, something we rarely have time or need to do in detail for other children. This was because we thought we needed to be specific when we recommended the child psychologist, or worse case, when we might have to ask that Kurt be withdrawn from our program.

At times families don't agree
and we have to make hard decisions.

You can't always succeed; don't be afraid to refer. We use the rule of thumb — *would we be remiss if* — we didn't recommend or share something. In Kurt's case, we felt it important to let his parents know his behavior was out of the ordinary and would surely be a problem for him in kindergarten where there was nowhere near the staffing ratio that we were able to provide. We recognized our limits, we are not child psychologists, and we recommended a referral. Given that our advice was not taken, we needed to be content with the belief that we were providing as psychologically healthy a situation as we could during the times the child was at our school.

THOUGHTS FOR PARENTS

Let's try to understand how a child sees himself in his environment.

A child's behavior is based on his understanding of reality, his perception of his environment and his place in it. As I mentioned in the case of Janelle, we can't change a child's behavior for him (or her), but we can work on the child's perception, so that *he* can change his behavior. As children gain in cognitive awareness, it is natural for them to compare themselves with others around them. A youngest child in a family of active, physical children often cannot compete physically and may feel there is no role, no use for him. He or she may imitate the older children's behaviors and words and may pick on younger children in a way he perceives himself picked on. We can try to be aware of how a child sees herself/himself in the family and think about ways we might help children feel strengths and realize that they have special talents and help develop them.

Using rewards to extinguish angry behavior may backfire.

There are specific behaviors that occasionally can be changed by a reward system; for instance, forgetting to hang up a coat, to make a bed. But anger? How can we change this with a reward? I feel that the reason some reward systems work in the short term is because for many families, this is the first time they have sat down with the child and clearly defined what the expected behavior is. Making a list of things *not* to do is okay, if it helps the child know what the family or school limits are. Of course, a list of what to do *instead* is also necessary. And once that's done, the rewards are usually beside the point, and certainly not part of a respectful family relationship. Still, for some families they work, especially if the children are involved in setting up the system and are willing parties to it, so they don't feel too manipulated.

Teaching to Individual Differences

Anger often means a lack of control.

Feeling manipulated is exactly why some children show anger. An angry child often means a scared child, a child who feels no control, who feels or believes that he or she is powerless to cause an effect. Anger develops, people react, and often children learn that angry behavior becomes a way they *can* have power, a way that they can control. Of course, there are many adults who control others with anger, but this is not considered healthy for relationships. It's important that children who are exhibiting undue anger and the inability or unwillingness to control anger receive some kind of help.

Early perceptions can make a lifelong difference.

The years of early childhood are the times when children form a perception of themselves, as in "I'm a good kid," "I'm a helping person," "I can figure things out," or in "When I'm mad, watch out," or "No one likes me." These early perceptions can stay with people and become self-fulfilling in the long term regardless of later successes or failures. If our child is exhibiting behavior that is causing difficulties at home and at school, and as parents we feel we've tried everything, we need to look for help with behavioral psychologists as recommended by pediatricians or school psychologists. There are well-researched ways to help children learn more positive self-perceptions, and help them gain resilience and self-control.

Michael: "Well, hello, George!"

MICHAEL CAME OUT OF THE CAR with that jerky, fast gait, Dad following behind with a backpack and a smile. "Hi, George," he called to one of the children sitting on the split rail fence at the school parking lot. "Well, hello, George," he waved with a big grin at the little girl just getting out of her car.

His dad gave him a hug and was on his way. Michael walked toward the fence to sit next to the teacher, Mary. "Hi, George," he said as he reached out his hand for a waiting high five. I thought it was really neat the way he greeted the children now, he looked so glad to see them. However, this being difficult, he somehow got the idea to call them all George.

"Hi, Michael, I'm Mary," answered the cheerful teacher, returning the high five. "You can go over and sit next to Caroline and David, too," accentuating the names for emphasis as she pointed to each child.

I thought of the progress Michael had made this year, as I watched him sitting with the arriving children. Last fall, he had wandered all around the lot and his aide had to keep bringing him back over, sometimes pulling and tugging him, telling him again and again, "All the kids are here, come sit with the kids ..."

Kids? What were kids? He had seemed not to notice, sometimes even bumping into them in his hurry to get to the barnyard where he would reach out, touch the goat or the sheep, then shrink back, shrieking, as the aide coaxed his hand again toward the patient animal. When we'd call the children together for story or singing, he'd race 'round and 'round the group. He got so excited he needed to be held, cuddled, and rocked by the nearest teacher to calm him down.

It had been such a long time since I've last seen him do that repetitive rocking and chewing on his fist. We'd come and hold him and massage his back to help him settle. He had stopped that behavior once his folks dismissed his aide and his mother came to be with him at school. She was more able to read his needs and to know when Michael, well, Michael was being 'Fragile X' again.

"Just one little part of a chromosome," his mom, Miriam, would say. "So nearly perfect, but not quite. Poor Michael." She smiled at him with adoration, obviously loving him just as he was, and ready to fight for every opportunity to optimize the potential she so clearly saw in him.

It had been her idea to have him join the class here at the Farm this year. His older brother had attended a few years back, and Miriam and Rob believed that the outdoor emphasis, the physical exercise, and care of animals would be ideal for their child labeled "autistic, developmentally delayed." It took a bit of convincing for the special education consultants from her school district. They did not agree that 'mainstreaming,' as they called it then, was the right road for Michael. This child needed one-on-one attention and a structured environment, they were certain. But Miriam had read everything she could find about children with Fragile X syndrome, and what stuck in her mind was that "Imitation was the way they learned." Michael would watch other people and imitate them, even if he didn't often care to communicate with them. "And if he's with other delayed children, he'll just imitate them," she exclaimed. "He needs to be with regular kids, I know he'll do better!"

Our staff agreed to give it a try. Accommodating our program to fit his needs hadn't been too difficult. A new, higher latch was placed on the barn door, since Michael, tall at five years old and adept with his fingers, loved to open the door and run into the barn, heading for the hayloft. We tried not having one special teacher for him, so he wouldn't come to expect one-on-one attention, but the reality was that we always had one teacher ready to be there beside him, especially outdoors, where limits such as fences and gates didn't seem to stop him. More than once a teacher took off sprinting after a spirited Michael who'd decided to run after that flying pigeon or darting kitten.

Now it was almost springtime, after an increasingly successful winter during which his mom coached him in getting used to the other children around him. Michael had learned to join in sledding with the others, he sat with us as we sang songs, and would look rapturously at books during large group story times, as long as he could be right up front, sometimes even pointing to the words. Recently we had found a third teacher who could be an extra help for us, and his mother stopped coming. She wanted to see him learn to be without her and to be successful in a mainstream program. Her goal was simple, "At least some part of kindergarten, I want him in with the regular kids!"

It was while he looked at books that we saw him begin to notice the other children. He liked paging through each picture book, calling out words as he turned the pages. Soon he was joining others at the book corner, looking at books with them and a teacher. He also repeatedly visited the art table, having learned to write a big M, and drawing the same smiley face with the M below it. The other children were impressed. Michael was actually a year older than most of the children, and making a face was pretty advanced for some of the "threes" and "fours' who were still making circles and lines and colors at random. They had tolerated him outdoors, knowing that somehow he needed extra help, but as children often do, not really paying much attention to him, because he didn't seem to notice them, either. But now, sitting at the art table or book corner, he began talking to them. Michael was interesting!

"Poopy, poopy, butt, butt ..." he'd blurt out. Giggles from the other children. Wow, this was fun, thought Michael. "Poop, doop, loop, poop," he'd try again. Now, every four-year-old knows this is just about the funniest thing to say, and something they'd dare not say in public themselves. They'd laugh, he'd smile. Soon they were trying to get him to say it again.

Needless to say, the teachers were hoping for another avenue of communication, even if this was a beginning. Our tactic was to take his word literally, and whenever he would say the "P" word, we'd solicitously lead him to the bathroom, saying things like, "Well, you'd better go right in to the bathroom. Come on, I'll help you hurry over." Once in the bathroom we'd say, "Oh, I thought you had to go." "No," Michael would say, and then we'd come back with him to the table, where we'd divert the discussion to the M on his paper or the face on his picture.

After several weeks of this tactic, the bathroom words disappeared, and he began saying "hi" to the kids and try other words, some of which actually made sense. The contact with children was beginning to pay off, we observed. He watched them and imitated them as they played in the cardboard space ship, the play grocery store and especially, the pretend library. He'd pick out book after book to bring up to the desk to pretend to take out of the library. "I want to take out this book. Can you stamp it?" This was a high point of his interaction with the pretend librarians.

I remember that exchange distinctly, because I videotaped it, along with pictures of Michael listening to a story and joining in on group snack and singing. I was hoping to build a convincing witness for Miriam to use at the year's end IEP meeting (IEP stands for Individual Educational Program, a report mandated by the state Department of Education) That meeting was to decide his case about kindergarten next year. Maybe today I would bring out the camera again as we counted votes for the new lamb, I thought, as I watched the children at their play. "George, come here ..." I heard him say. Oh, there's that George calling again, I lamented silently.

It was actually a sign of progress that as he began noticing and wishing to interact with other children, he wanted to call them by name. This being difficult, however, he had somehow got the idea to call them all George. Again, the children thought this was hysterical (not quite as risqué as the P word, but, funny anyway.) The more they'd laugh, the more he'd call them George again, as if this was his ticket to popularity. While his teachers celebrated Michael's desire to be interacting with his new friends, we weren't quite comfortable with them laughing at him. We modeled sensitivity and respect. When he'd call them George, we'd quickly and calmly interject, "Her name is Olivia," or "This is Justin."

I was sitting at the art table with Michael later that day when I reminded him, once again, that a certain person was not George, but really had a different name. Molly, an observant five-year-old, looked up from her coloring and suggested, as if to help, "Why don't you just ask him to go to the bathroom?" Amazing! She had noticed our original tactic on the P word and thought that maybe it would work for Michael on the George issue as well. Now, all the kids weren't this insightful, but Molly's comment reinforced my belief that the children were aware of their teachers' intent in helping Michael on this learning task. Day by day, while Michael often persisted in calling each of them George at some time or another, the laughing had been diminishing, and the children began reminding him of their names themselves, as though they all wanted him, really, to learn their real names.

Then it was time for clean-up and to meet at the large chart at the end of the Big Room, where teacher Mary was calling the group together to vote on the names for the new lambs. I wasn't sure Michael would understand the entire process, but neither did many of the younger children in the group. It was one of those multileveled learning activities. Three-year-olds gained some inkling of the importance of their initial or mark on a piece of paper, and of the idea that we could all work together to decide an issue, while the older children in the group were learning to read the names and count the votes.

Michael had not quite mastered the skill of sitting down for reasons that weren't immediately obvious to him, so I sat behind him, snuggling with him a bit, and rocking him from time to time, while he watched and listened to the explanations. One by one the children walked to the chart, where the teacher handed them a marker, and they would make a line beside the large printed name they preferred. After several names had been called, the teacher called, "Michael, it's your turn to vote." He stood up and walked to the front, reached out for the marker, and, imitating or understanding, made a clear mark under just one name, his vote. Then he came back to sit with me.

Oh, where was that camera? I was too busy to record the scene, but I will remember it, and tell of it, forever. It wasn't important if he understood all of it, but that day, Michael was definitely an involved and accepted 'voting' member of the class.

THOUGHTS FOR TEACHERS

Teachers plan for individual differences in all children.

Welcoming a child with special needs into a classroom may seem daunting, until we remember that all children have particular and individual needs, and they cover a wide range. Teaching young children in a multi-age-group class is clearly one that involves dealing with all kinds of individual differences. This understanding of what we do best can give us the confidence to know that, of course, we will be able to accommodate a child labeled 'different.'

If possible, avoid having the child perceive that he has a one-to-one aide.

If it is necessary, and sometimes it clearly is, to have an extra staff person to 'track' or help the child with more challenging needs, it is still important that ALL staff be seen by the child as his teachers. We have seen well-intentioned aides, like the first assistant for Michael, devote themselves too clearly to that one child, so that the game for the child becomes one of getting the attention of his or her special teacher. Michael's mother was skilled at seeing when he needed help, but not overdoing, and at inserting Michael into situations with other children and talking with all of them, so that he gradually became comfortable with the children around him and then she could give less and less help. After a month or two we were able to 'mainstream' Michael to the extent that he really didn't have a special teacher, but all the teachers spelled each other at working with Michael if he needed it, or at 'tracking' him outdoors, for safety issues. This intentional strategy of shared assistance has proven to be the most successful way of using that extra teacher to the benefit of the child' growth, as opposed to merely supervision.

**All children can benefit from learning about
and accepting individual differences.**

When a child is clearly different in a group it does not need
to be a problem. Instead, it offers another educational
opportunity. Not only did Michael need to see and be with
'regular' children, so did the other children need to begin to
be aware of differences in people. They needed to learn to
be accepting and understanding of people with challenging
disabilities, people who acted differently and sometimes
even downright strangely. The challenge became one of
giving Michael the help he needed while still helping the
other children learn about individual differences. We didn't
want to allow the children to laugh at his "George" calling,
and yet, they were children. How could we expect them to
be socially sensitive and politically correct? I think the
answer lay in our continued modeling of respect and the
teaching strategies oriented toward a specific problem,
which the children could see were effective. We were careful
not to single out Michael as different or difficult, any more
than we would single out the child with sharing problems or
shyness problems. Molly's comment showed us that the
strategy was working. She went a step further to propose an
idea for helping us accomplish it!

THOUGHTS FOR PARENTS

They are all 'special.'

Parents of children with 'special needs' can do well to remind themselves that all children are 'special.' They all have specific needs. If a child finds it challenging to settle down at group time, it helps to know that other "regular" children also have difficulties at group time, at sharing, at taking the point of view of another. All these individual differences can and will be taken into account by our child's teachers. We are not asking for too much when we discuss the individual needs of our child with the teachers. It is our job to know our child best, and to advocate for him or her. On the other hand, in the classroom safety and learning of *all* children are the concerns of teachers; they are always trying to balance the needs of a 'special' child with the needs of each individual child they care for as well as the needs of the whole group of children. This is what makes up the challenging and interesting job of teaching. We each have different roles and can respect each other's viewpoints in these roles.

Modeling respect and understanding starts at home.

What can we say when our child comes home giggling about the silly things a schoolmate says or does? Modeling respect and dealing with individual differences starts at home. We can ask, "I wonder why he does that?" or "Do you think he understands those words?" or "Maybe for some people it is harder to remember names like you can …" After a while our child begins to realize there are many ways that people are different.

The next step to noticing the ways people are different could be to think of how we could help. "I wonder if we reminded him of our names, he'd remember better?"

Our children will grow up living in a world of immense variation in individual differences. We can teach caring and constructive noticing of differences, hand in hand with the continued appreciation of all the ways we are the same, as in "Look, Michael loves to look at books, too." Through our own conversations and actions, we can encourage a sensitive and caring human being in our child.

Part 4: Teaching Compassion and Caring

Brandon: "But I'm not hungry."

*Helping a child with the 'me-first' mentality
to recognize the needs of others.*

IT WAS FEEDING TIME on the first day of a summer class at the farm, and Brandon just didn't get it. There he went, running toward the sheep, with intern teacher Katie bolting behind, calling, "Brandon, over here, we're feeding the chickens now. Please stay with us." The brown-eyed three-year-old, sturdy legs churning as he pointed, seemed not to hear her.

"Lookit, sheep!" said Brandon. Observing the barnyard as Summer Program Director, I gently turned him around and directed him over toward the coop. "There's your group. They need you over there to help feed the chickens."

"Oh, chickens," he cooed, and ran back toward Katie and the other four children. She began to show them how to softly throw the feed through the fence into their feeder.

"See, they look hungry," the teacher counseled encouragingly. But Brandon was not interested in watching them eat. After a small handful toss, he noticed the goats across the way, and darted toward them. Katie called him, but it took a run-after and a hand-hold to bring him back again. The other children walked together purposefully toward baaing and clucking charges, while Brandon shifted from pen to pen, unable to decide which he'd feed first or to remember where his group was going next.

Then it was time to water them. Each child learned how to push his bucket under the big old-style hand pump and push the handle up and down until the water pulled up through the pipe and emerged, miraculously, through the effort of their own muscles. Proudly they staggered with their overfull and sloshing buckets, toward the waiting troughs or tanks. The pigs rushed to the fountain's edge as the children listened to their gurgles and smacks. But Brandon was not interested in watching them drink; he was off toward the barn this time, teacher on his heels.

At last the animals were fed, watered, and petted. It was time to play at the climber and sandbox, paint pictures, ride the pony, and plant a garden. I resolved to check in with Katie after the morning class to see how Brandon coped.

I found Katie resting, feet up on the small chairs in the schoolroom/ teacher lunchroom. "Oh, he coped, all right. He just wanted to do it all ... his way!" Here's how she recalled it:

He wanted to be first at the pony ride. He refused to wait for the person in front of him, and wiggled in past her, only to be reminded that he'd be next, that he could keep playing and everyone would get a chance. "But I want a ride," was his response.

He wanted to water his garden before he put the seeds in. Even as she showed him how to hold the seeds carefully and sprinkle them on the fluffy soil, he dropped the seeds to grab the water can. "But I wanta water."

And at snack time, he wanted his snack. Right then. The snack was passed around the circle of waiting children who were seated on a blanket. Brandon grabbed the bucket of apples, took his, and kept the bucket on his lap. "Brandon, the person next to you wants an apple, too."

"But I want a apple."

Katie summed it up. "I may be wrong, but I think he'll take a while to get the hang of things here."

Sure enough, the next day, Brandon raced happily down the hill with his group toward the baaing and clucking animals. Then he took a turn toward the play area, heading determinedly toward that nifty climber he enjoyed yesterday, when his teacher called, "Brandon, we're all over here."

"Huh?"

"We're feeding the animals now. They need their food," a patient Katie explained.

"But I'm not hungry," countered Brandon. Logically, to him.

"The chickens are hungry. They need us. And the pigs ..." the teacher waved toward the barnyard, where the other children were already picking up the labeled feed buckets and starting to pump water into plastic buckets.

"... Oh ... chickens ... oh ..." Brandon joined the group.

It still wasn't an easy day, but there was some improvement as Brandon began seeing the routine, to notice the other children, and to hear the words of explanation and encouragement being offered. At day's end, we gave his mother an idea of what we were working on with him.

Not surprised, Brandon's mother laughed. "He's not a bad kid. He's just, basically, clueless ..." (Her words. She thought it was cute!) "Of course, he doesn't understand about helping, I mean, he's only three! We just want him to have a good time."

THOUGHTS FOR TEACHERS

Parents' expectations may not be the same as ours.

Children come to us not only with varying capabilities, but from families with their own goals and visions of what their children should and could be. Brandon's mother clearly had different expectations for how he should be acting. She claimed, "But he's *only* three," and I was thinking, but he's *already* three.

It's important to know the child development studies and what we can expect from children at different stages.

Teachers can, however, differentiate between values/beliefs, and scientific evidence about what children can think or achieve. Research about learning and motivation can inform educators about what to expect children are capable of at certain ages. For instance, we know that children as young as eighteen months can learn to take the point of view of others and act in their interest. (In one study by Gopnik, children fed their teachers broccoli, knowing they liked it, even though they themselves chose crackers. That's not clueless!) We observe that by three-years-old healthy children will look around when their name is called and respond, if not immediately, to words like 'come' and 'stop,' and they definitely watch other children for clues.

Yet many educational studies tell of the power of expectations, which can become self-fulfilling prophecies. I am concerned that with more families either not taking the time, or caring, to raise caring children, teachers find themselves dealing with these children, and then determining the capabilities of the whole group from the egocentric children they see. The 'dumbing down' of curriculum takes place at this age at the social/emotional level, in not asking children to take care of their own basic needs or to begin thinking of the needs of others. Bribes, manipulation, and power-wielding become 'management strategies,' with the sad loss of children's opportunities for real social/emotional growth.

Schools can plan for age-appropriate social/emotional growth.

The farm has proven to be an especially useful setting for helping children to de-center. Animals can be a helpful, motivating step toward learning to care about others. Instead of it being 'all about me,' we can shift the focus to, "What can I do to help those animals; what can I do to work and play together with these children; what should I do to belong here?" It wouldn't have to be a farm. Classroom pets, plants to water, cooking or constructing jobs, helping to set up play areas, to sweep up after sand play; these could also provide motivating ways to begin to de-center, to think about the needs of the situation and how to be useful.

When parental goals differ from ours, we understand their goals are for their children to be happy; we try showing the children that happiness can be more than "What I can get someone to do for me," but instead, "What I can do for someone else." We respect family and cultural differences, but we won't change our expectations for kids, which are based on our knowledge of what children can do, joyfully, every day at the Children's Farm.

THOUGHTS FOR PARENTS

If we don't ask, we may not know
what a child's capabilities are.

How do we judge the capabilities of our children? The miracle of the hand pump comes to mind here. Who knew that by pushing the handle up and down water would come out? And once they saw they could, those children became really competent at pumping, just as their three-year-old ancestors were a hundred years ago. By the same logic, if we don't ask them to come when called, or to think of the needs of others, how will they learn that they can? What else are they capable of that because of safety, convenience, or time constraints of our modern age, we simply don't ask them to do?

Some parents are concerned about discouraging children by asking them to do too much. Surely this is the case with neglected or abused children, children who are working just to stay alive and stay safe. But the children in many Middle American homes are rarely challenged or expected to meet their potential. They may be taught to count, to recognize colors and letters, but perhaps not those important words like 'help,' 'we need you,' and 'he's hungry, too.'

Families can provide
age-appropriate challenges for children.

Of course, most children have times when they just don't want to stop, they wish they hadn't heard their name called, and they really don't want to share or take turns. We understand, yet keep expecting, just as we had known they'd learn to walk, even though they fell. Teachers use the word "scaffolding," which means challenging children at a little higher level than where they are comfortable, as an important way to guide them. If we ask, then show and explain, allow for a few setbacks but continue to challenge them, children will be encouraged, not discouraged.

Discouragement comes when we do things for them that they can do for themselves, or when we don't believe in their capabilities. Allowing them to fail at a task helps them learn resilience and courage.

Families are a great place to learn awareness of others.

Living in a family for three years means that words and expectations have been absorbed to some degree. By this time, most children have also begun to realize that other people have thoughts and feelings. That's what families can teach best. Yet a child who has someone at his beck and call, who doesn't need to think about what to do next, who only needs to think about what he wants next, will not learn the skills of being in any other setting than the one in which he is the center. If parents see their role as 'doing for' and 'keeping happy,' there may be little incentive to teach concepts of self-control and awareness of others.

We can let our child know we're hungry, too, and that she can do something to help us, as in 'pass the snack.' And when we help others, we can include our child in the action. We can ask him to help feed the dog or teach his sister a task. Use the 'we' word, as in "How can we help?" so that he will learn that being helpful is an expectation for all.

Making sure the child is 'happy' at all times does not necessarily guide the child toward the goal of becoming a thinking, cooperating member of a community of learners. The words, "but I'm not hungry" are too often the sentiments of the privileged of the world — attitudes that can be replaced, if begun early enough, with words of "Oh look, they need me, I can help." Parents, as all caretakers, create the future of the world, one human being at a time.

Ruby: "Oh, I know ... I felt that way, too!"

A caring child teaches us, once again,
the cognitive and social capabilities of children.

WE WERE HEADING OUT with the class for a short walk on one of the beginning days of the school year. The children moved at different speeds, some racing ahead to be first at the log circle 'waiting place,' others slowly checking out the ants in the grass or the flowers at the side. One three-year-old girl didn't want to move at all. She whimpered and whined softly, tears building up in her eyes.

Hmm ... she had such a good first day, I thought. *Is she concerned because we're leaving the familiar area heading to an 'unknown' on the hike? Is she worried about keeping up with the faster moving children? Did she wish for a friend but hasn't found one yet?*

Then I heard her words, "Mama, Mama," slowly and quietly as she tried to hold herself together.

I reached out my hand to her, offering a little support, and silently kept walking with her, hoping the mood would vanish as she became interested in the hike. Four-year-old Ruby came along beside us on the path.

"Why is she crying?" she asked me. I was about to answer, 'Well, she misses her mom,' but then I stopped. *This is a good learning moment.*

"I don't know, but you could ask her."

143

Ruby turned, "Why are you crying?"

"I ... I ... m ... m ... miss my mom," a quiet voice answered.

Oh, I *know* ..." Ruby said passionately, waving her arms. "I felt that way, too." (This was her second year.) "But it's okay, this is a good place!"

She reached out for the small hand, and together they walked ahead of me up the path to meet the rest of the class.

THOUGHTS FOR TEACHERS

Children can make rational deductions from observing others.

If we teach with the Piaget mindset that younger children cannot understand another person's point of view (so they will, of course, act selfishly) or with the mindset that young children, possessed with a human 'selfish gene' are not capable of caring for others unless we teach (or bribe) them, we may not give ourselves the chance to SEE this marvelous ability of the human mind.

Studies by cognitive and developmental psychologists have shown the remarkable ability of young children to observe others, make generalities, deduce ideas and emotions about others, and if encouraged (or permitted), follow through with caring actions. Observe, think, generalize, decide, act ... this is what humans can do.

Here's an example of true altruism: thinking, caring, and sharing.

The children were saying goodbye in the parking lot at the end of the day. One by one they waved to teachers and friends and climbed into their waiting min-vans or carpools. As his friends left, Joseph was left sitting by himself on the end bench. Teacher Vicky moved over to sit nearer to him.

"You must have thought I was feeling lonesome," said Joseph.

Another teacher 'wow' moment. A three-year-old showed he was capable of thinking about what someone else was thinking about what he might be thinking! In other words, one mind deduced the thoughts of another mind, and voiced it back.

Unless we teach it out of them ...

Answering questions too quickly, not asking children to voice their thoughts, and assuming they will need us to speak for them and tell them what to notice, are often actions of well-meaning teachers of young children. Our own 'mindsets' about the capabilities of children, our insistence on order and routine, or our own needs to feel useful as teachers can interfere. In the case of Ruby's caring question, I could have said, "Well, I'll tell you why she's crying." Then I would have felt like a useful, needed teacher ... but missed the chance to learn.

Reminding myself that teaching involves observing, listening, and learning the capabilities of children as well as talking to them, I will never forget Ruby's thoughtful words.

THOUGHTS FOR PARENTS

Altruism involves thinking, feeling, and caring.

Developmental psychologist Alison Gopnik describes the steps children go through as learners: from observing, thinking, and hypothesizing, to acting. Her research also demonstrates that they can learn to act in a caring way. Her famous broccoli study showed children giving broccoli to the adult researchers because they observed that the adults liked it. Other similar studies show children as early as fourteen months helping an experimenter get a pen that is out of the adult's reach, even toddling across the room to get there when the child observes the teacher's need.

Altruism: It's more than caring or feeling; it's acting on our sympathies and empathies to alleviate someone else's pain even if we don't feel it ourselves.

We were all sitting around a circle, eating muffins we had just baked together. It was almost the end of the class before spring break. Children were sharing their plans for the next week. Teacher Jenny commented to the children near her that she was going on a long car trip right after school. The boy next to her, looking concerned, said, "You'll get hungry; here, take mine." And he held out his muffin to her.

As parents, we can demonstrate daily to our children how we care for them, and of course we do, but we can also include expectations for them to be caring and to act in caring ways. "Look, baby sister feels bad; how can we help her?" and "Daddy looks tired; let's see if he wants a little help with that ladder." These are ways we can include our children in daily family processes of figuring out the needs of others. Thanks and hugs are also better than 'good job' on a helpful task, because these demonstrations pay attention to the benefits of the action the child has just completed.

Children learn from their peers as well.

Child development studies also inform us about how

children observe and emulate other children. If given a choice to watch adults or other children, they choose the child. In addition to family members, peer groups can be useful in helping children de-center, starting with a friend, a helpful one, or one who needs a little help that an older child can provide. Then finding a small play group or preschools that foster social-emotional learning and encourage children to help each other, can make a difference in how children see and act with other children. When looking for a play group, daycare, or school, we can ask, "Is it competitive? Too many children? Too many rules and not enough free play and peer interaction?" These are some questions I would ask people to consider, rather than just, "Are there cheery teachers who help children to 'have fun'"?

The Children's Farm provides an interesting, motivating place to learn all kinds of things, where we value the social-emotional learning as basic foundations to the other amazing steps in a growing child's capabilities. We wish that all children can find a place where they will tell their friends, "This is a good place."

Nancy Jones

Acknowledgments

ANY ACKNOWLEDGEMENT for contributions to this book must begin with Dave Jones. Early in our life raising children on a small farm, he saw the value of the learning happening here.

After a particularly enjoyable summer of working and learning in the garden with our two-and four-year-olds, Dave said, "I know, Nan, we should have a school right here on the farm!"

"Oh, no, I couldn't … I'm exhausted as it is …"

"Oh, you wouldn't need to be the teacher, you'd be the director," he said.

Well, it took a bit more time, but eventually, as I researched early childhood education, participated in child development classes at the local technical college, and began networking with other teachers and parents of young children, the idea took hold.

The words of Rudolf Dreikurs in *Children the Challenge* on the needs of children and the importance of being useful truly resonated as we watched our young children help in the garden, care for kittens, and gather and count eggs on the farm.

We saw that 'whole-child learning' was very possible in nature and farm activities, and often much more motivating as an appropriate way to learn for young children. We began with two five-week summer classes the year 1974 and opened the nursery school in September 1976.

Dave began planning for an addition to our farmhouse that would be spacious enough for a classroom on the lower level; he literally pounded in every nail for that first building and every addition since. He also maintained the farm buildings and added on new coops and fences as needed. This school owes so much to Dave's work and support, not just the building support but emotional support, encouragement, and good ideas throughout the years.

I am grateful for the inspiration, examples, and help from our children, Ann, Patty, Carrie, and Barb, who lived through the developing curriculum, and who continue offering support and advice to our school Board of Directors.

All our teachers have contributed so much to the curriculum and philosophy, beginning with Regina Buono, our first teacher who brought her experience and intelligence to the first twelve years of our school. Other huge contributors and participants in the 'stories' I have presented here are Carol Incremona, Mary Stahlmann, Sam Horak, Mitzi Brown, Jenny Hanlon, and Jenny Jacobson, as well as numerous intern teachers who have contributed to our summer programs. A thank-you to Carol Incremona for her early editing of several chapters, and to Carrie Magee for her help and support in reading and commenting on this book over the years.

I'd also like to thank editor Jami Carpenter and photographer Pete Vordenberg who have encouraged me this past year in my efforts to assemble this book.

I have been fortunate to live at a time and place where I can learn from children what it is to be human … for *children are like that*.

About the Author

NANCY JONES started her teaching career as a high school French teacher and then embarked on her most interesting teaching experience with her husband, Dave, raising their family of four children. She returned to college to study child development at the University of Minnesota, earning her teaching credentials for Early Childhood, then went on to pursue a master's degree in Parent Education and Child Development (Child and Family Studies) at St. Cloud State University. Nancy started the Children's Farm School in 1976 and has been actively involved as director, teacher, and parent educator. She currently lives on the farm in Minnesota and continues to learn from the children and teachers at the school.

www.ingramcontent.com/pod-product-compliance
Lightning Source LLC
Chambersburg PA
CBHW071223090426
42736CB00014B/2957